McCALL-CRABBS

Standard Test Lessons in Reading

Book C

WILLIAM A. McCALL, Ph.D.
Professor Emeritus of Education
Teachers College, Columbia University

LELAH CRABBS SCHROEDER, Ph.D.
Formerly Assistant Professor of Education
Teachers College, Columbia University

Revised under the editorial supervision of
ROBERT P. STARR. Ed.D.

Teachers College, Columbia University
New York and London

Copyright © 1979 by Teachers College, Columbia University.
All rights reserved. Earlier editions © 1926, 1950, 1961,
copyright © 1978 by Teachers College, Columbia University.
Published by Teachers College Press, 1234 Amsterdam Avenue,
New York, NY 10027.

No part of this publication may be reproduced or transmitted in any form or by any
means, electronic or mechanical, including photocopy, recording, or any information
retrieval system, without written permission of the publisher.

Printed in the United States of America
ISBN: 5544-3

15 14 13 12 11   20 19 18 17

"Ding-dong!" sounded the fire bell, and away rushed Fred and John. Three hours later the two boys returned much sobered by the sights they had seen. The largest apartment house in the city had burned to the ground, and many people had been made homeless. The fire started on the third floor, where an electric iron had been left turned on.

The boys talked about the causes of fires. Fred had read that electricity used carelessly causes many fires. Carelessness with matches, usually on the part of smokers, is another frequent cause of fires.

1. **The boys rushed away to the** Ⓐ game Ⓑ fire Ⓒ fight Ⓓ show
2. **They returned in about** Ⓐ one hour Ⓑ two hours Ⓒ three hours Ⓓ four hours
3. **Fred and John came back feeling** Ⓐ gay Ⓑ sad Ⓒ sobered Ⓓ tired
4. **The fire started** Ⓐ in the basement Ⓑ in the kitchen Ⓒ on the roof Ⓓ on the third floor
5. **The fire was caused by** Ⓐ matches Ⓑ a bad flue Ⓒ an electric iron Ⓓ a stove
6. **The boys talked about** Ⓐ the fire Ⓑ causes of fires Ⓒ firemen Ⓓ the people
7. **Fires from matches are usually caused by** Ⓐ boys Ⓑ mice Ⓒ smokers Ⓓ cats
8. **What was first mentioned as a cause of fire?** Ⓐ carelessness Ⓑ matches Ⓒ gasoline Ⓓ rubbish

No. right	1	2	3	4	5	6	7	8
G score	2.3	2.6	3.1	3.7	4.3	4.8	5.6	6.5

2

In the Netherlands and Belgium, children do not have their fun and presents on Christmas Day. They go to church on Christmas Day, and they have their fun on St. Nicholas Day, which comes on December 6. The night before, they fix something to hold their gifts. Sometimes it is a well-polished shoe, sometimes a plate or a basket, and sometimes they hang up their stockings. St. Nicholas rides a gray horse or a white donkey, and so the children leave water for the animal to drink and something for it to eat. They leave hay, oats, or a carrot, and sometimes a piece of bread. In the morning, if they have been good, they find that St. Nicholas has left sweets, fruits, and playthings for them.

1. **On what day of the month does St. Nicholas Day come?** Ⓐ the 6th Ⓑ the 8th Ⓒ the 9th Ⓓ the 25th
2. **What does St. Nicholas sometimes ride?** Ⓐ a white horse Ⓑ a gray horse Ⓒ a gray donkey Ⓓ reindeer
3. **When do the children in the story receive presents?** Ⓐ Christmas Day Ⓑ New Year's Eve Ⓒ St. Nicholas Day Ⓓ December 25
4. **At what season of the year does this holiday come?** Ⓐ winter Ⓑ spring Ⓒ summer Ⓓ fall
5. **Sometimes they use a plate** Ⓐ for the horse Ⓑ for the bread Ⓒ to hold their gifts Ⓓ as a gift
6. **They leave water** Ⓐ for the animal Ⓑ for St. Nicholas Ⓒ in the plate Ⓓ for children
7. **Candy is left for** Ⓐ the horse Ⓑ the mule Ⓒ everyone Ⓓ good children
8. **St. Nicholas leaves** Ⓐ baskets Ⓑ toys Ⓒ carrots Ⓓ bread

No. right	1	2	3	4	5	6	7	8
G score	2.1	2.5	2.9	3.6	4.3	5.1	6.0	7.0

Did you know that your mouth is like a little mill? Your teeth grind your food. The front teeth are shaped to bite the food into bits. The others are made to grind it fine so that it can be made into liquid by the stomach. Children have twenty-four teeth, but adults have thirty-two. Enamel is the hard outer covering on the teeth. To crack nuts with your teeth might break this enamel, and it will not grow a second time. Down in the middle of the tooth is a nerve. When the enamel is broken, this nerve feels the heat or cold. Soon the tooth begins to ache. If you want this mill of yours to work well for a long time, you must take good care of it.

3

1. **How many teeth do children usually have?** Ⓐ 16　Ⓑ 20　Ⓒ 24　Ⓓ 32
2. **How many teeth do most grown people have?** Ⓐ 16　Ⓑ 20　Ⓒ 24　Ⓓ 32
3. **On the outside of the teeth there is** Ⓐ enamel　Ⓑ bone　Ⓒ muscle　Ⓓ a nerve
4. **In the center of the teeth are** Ⓐ enamel　Ⓑ bone　Ⓒ muscle　Ⓓ nerves
5. **The enamel on the teeth is** Ⓐ soft　Ⓑ cold　Ⓒ hard　Ⓓ liquid
6. **The front teeth** Ⓐ bite food　Ⓑ grind food　Ⓒ soften food　Ⓓ chew food
7. **If the enamel is once broken, when does new enamel form?** Ⓐ in a few days　Ⓑ in a few weeks　Ⓒ in a few years　Ⓓ never
8. **This is a lesson in** Ⓐ geography　Ⓑ health　Ⓒ history　Ⓓ arithmetic

No. right	1	2	3	4	5	6	7	8
G score	2.4	2.7	3.4	3.9	4.6	5.3	6.1	7.0

4

Who would ever have thought that the old trolley car, with its bell clanging for joy, might return to our city streets? Your grandparents could tell you that most trolleys were long ago replaced by buses and cars.

What's wrong with buses and cars? If everyone used private cars, our city streets would become choked with traffic. Both buses and cars produce unhealthy air pollution. The government wants to find a new way to move lots of people quickly, cheaply, and quietly.

Since the trolley car runs on electricity, it is quiet and does not produce clouds of exhaust fumes. Shiny new trolley cars, which are called *light rail vehicles*, are now being built for many cities. Do not be surprised if older folks smile when they see this new "vehicle of the future" clanging down the street.

1. **Trolley cars**   Ⓐ are a new invention   Ⓑ were used many years ago   Ⓒ will never be used again   Ⓓ are found only in museums
2. **Most trolleys run on**   Ⓐ steam   Ⓑ coal   Ⓒ electricity   Ⓓ gasoline
3. **What is the best reason for using trolleys?**   Ⓐ they can reduce air pollution   Ⓑ they are old   Ⓒ they are fun to ride   Ⓓ they run on tracks
4. **One problem with using buses is that they**   Ⓐ are too small   Ⓑ cause traffic jams   Ⓒ help cause air pollution   Ⓓ do not have a bell
5. **Trolleys are now called**   Ⓐ light buses   Ⓑ heavy rail vehicles   Ⓒ rail buses   Ⓓ light rail vehicles
6. **This story says that most old trolleys**   Ⓐ remained in use   Ⓑ were replaced by buses and cars   Ⓒ were painted red   Ⓓ were too expensive
7. **Choose the best title:**   Ⓐ The End of the Line   Ⓑ The Happy Return of the Trolley   Ⓒ The History of Railroads   Ⓓ Private Cars Are the Answer
8. **According to this story**   Ⓐ cities are too large   Ⓑ cities should build more parks   Ⓒ old ideas sometimes give new solutions   Ⓓ older people should own cars

No. right	1	2	3	4	5	6	7	8
G score	2.7	3.3	3.7	4.2	4.7	5.4	6.0	6.7

Last summer I visited a lifesaving station. It is so named because the people stationed there are ready to save the lives of those who are in danger on the sea. When a ship is wrecked in a storm near the coast, the rescuers go out to save the crew and passengers. They use a large motorboat that is kept in one of the buildings. The boat is pushed out to the water on a low-wheeled truck. The front wheels are taken away by the guards, and the rest of the truck drops away by itself. Then the rescuers jump into the boat and are off to help those in danger. Every day they practice launching the boat quickly. This helps them speed to the rescue when someone needs their help.

5

1. **The rescue boat is launched from a**   Ⓐ dock   Ⓑ wreck   Ⓒ truck   Ⓓ ship

2. **This story is about a**   Ⓐ lighthouse   Ⓑ boathouse   Ⓒ training station   Ⓓ lifesaving station

3. **The boat is pushed out to the**   Ⓐ sand   Ⓑ beach   Ⓒ water   Ⓓ rocks

4. **The boat is kept**   Ⓐ in a building   Ⓑ in part of the house   Ⓒ on the ground   Ⓓ on the water

5. **The guards remove the**   Ⓐ runners   Ⓑ back wheels   Ⓒ front wheels   Ⓓ slidings

6. **The rescuers practice every**   Ⓐ month   Ⓑ year   Ⓒ day   Ⓓ hour

7. **The rescuers jump into the**   Ⓐ water   Ⓑ seaweed   Ⓒ boat   Ⓓ sand

8. **The rescuers save the**   Ⓐ ship in danger   Ⓑ food in the boat   Ⓒ fish in the sea   Ⓓ lives of people

No. right	1	2	3	4	5	6	7	8
G score	3.3	3.6	4.0	4.6	5.1	5.6	6.1	6.8

6

A little bird, a finch, was hovering over her young ones in a thorny bush when a hungry weasel saw them. He had caught nothing all night and was trying hard to get through the thorns to these little birds. At last he was near the nest. The mother bird trembled with fear, but she knew she must act quickly if she were to save her babies. She tumbled out of the nest and fell crying to the ground. The cry brought other birds, the jay, sparrow, and wren, but they could not help.

The weasel tried to get closer to the little birds, but the thorns stuck him again and again. The mother bird wished to make the weasel try to catch her so she fluttered about on the ground crying as if badly hurt. The weasel, seeing this, thought he could get a quick breakfast. He jumped down on the ground near her. She fluttered wildly along, keeping out of his grasp. After leading him far from her nest, the finch flew back to her young.

1. **The bird was a**   Ⓐ jay   Ⓑ finch   Ⓒ lark   Ⓓ wren
2. **Who was hungry?**   Ⓐ a rat   Ⓑ little birds   Ⓒ a finch   Ⓓ a weasel
3. **The weasel was having a hard time getting through the**   Ⓐ weeds   Ⓑ trees   Ⓒ birds   Ⓓ thorns
4. **The finch was**   Ⓐ asleep   Ⓑ afraid   Ⓒ happy   Ⓓ singing
5. **Who tumbled from the nest?**   Ⓐ little birds   Ⓑ a weasel   Ⓒ a finch   Ⓓ other birds
6. **Who came when the mother bird cried out?**   Ⓐ a hunter   Ⓑ other birds   Ⓒ a weasel   Ⓓ animals
7. **What did the finch do?**   Ⓐ fluttered about crying   Ⓑ fought   Ⓒ scolded   Ⓓ flew at the weasel
8. **The finch saved her babies by**   Ⓐ fighting   Ⓑ calling others   Ⓒ leading the weasel away   Ⓓ flying away

No. right	1	2	3	4	5	6	7	8
G score	2.5	2.9	3.5	4.1	4.7	5.5	6.3	7.1

Peter and Sara liked to fly. They lived in Los Angeles, and in the spring they flew to New York to visit their grandparents.

They had to be at the airport at 9:30 a.m., half an hour before departure time. When they had embarked a flight attendant helped them find their seats and fasten their seat belts. Peter sat next to the window and watched the luggage being loaded into the plane. He always tried to see his suitcase!

During the flight Sara and Peter played chess and read. After lunch Sara watched the movie.

The flight took five hours, and they arrived in New York at 6 p.m. eastern standard time. Peter's watch said 3 p.m. because of the three-hour time difference between New York and California. As he had an automatic watch, which told the date and the day of the week as well as the time, he decided not to change it.

1. **Peter and Sara visited their grandparents in**   Ⓐ the spring   Ⓑ the summer   Ⓒ the fall   Ⓓ the winter
2. **Their departure time was**   Ⓐ 8 a.m.   Ⓑ 9 a.m.   Ⓒ 10 a.m.   Ⓓ 11 a.m.
3. **Peter and Sara traveled**   Ⓐ with their parents   Ⓑ with their grandparents   Ⓒ by themselves   Ⓓ with friends
4. **Peter sat**   Ⓐ next to the pilot   Ⓑ next to the window   Ⓒ in the aisle seat   Ⓓ on the floor
5. **During the flight Peter and Sara played**   Ⓐ cards   Ⓑ chess   Ⓒ dominoes   Ⓓ snakes and ladders
6. **When they arrived in New York, Peter's watch said**   Ⓐ 3 p.m.   Ⓑ 4 p.m.   Ⓒ 5 p.m.   Ⓓ 6 p.m.
7. **The time difference between California and New York is**   Ⓐ one hour   Ⓑ three hours   Ⓒ five hours   Ⓓ there's no difference
8. **The direction Peter and Sara were traveling was**   Ⓐ west to east   Ⓑ east to west   Ⓒ north to south   Ⓓ south to north

No. right	1	2	3	4	5	6	7	8
G score	3.0	3.5	3.9	4.5	5.1	5.8	6.5	7.1

8

About 150 passengers climbed into the wooden coaches of the Duluth Limited, and the train rattled away into smoke from a far-off forest fire. These passengers rode for a long time. The train was approaching a town, but it never reached there. It was stopped by many people fleeing their homes. Beyond the town, the forest was a raging wall of flame. The conductor helped everyone into the train and started it racing backward as fast as the engineer could make it go. Could they outrun the raging fire? Could they make it back to Skunk Lake?

Suddenly the very air exploded into flames. The tops of the coaches caught fire. The wooden top of the engine cab began to burn. But the engineer and fireman remained at their posts.

The burning train outraced the forest fire. Everyone dashed from the train and into the waters of Skunk Lake. Bears and other wild animals shared the lake with them. From the safety of the water, they watched the forest fire race by and their train burn down to the engine and the wheels of the coaches.

---

1. **The engineer and fireman on this train were**   Ⓐ weak   Ⓑ tyrants   Ⓒ brave   Ⓓ sad
2. **There were about how many passengers?**   Ⓐ 130   Ⓑ 140   Ⓒ 150   Ⓓ 160
3. **The coaches were made of**   Ⓐ wood   Ⓑ steel   Ⓒ iron   Ⓓ aluminum
4. **The train never finished the trip because**   Ⓐ it got lost   Ⓑ the smoke was too thick   Ⓒ too many people boarded it   Ⓓ it burned
5. **The people escaped from the fire into**   Ⓐ Rabbit Creek   Ⓑ Skunk Lake   Ⓒ Bear Lake   Ⓓ Duluth River
6. **This story shows that**   Ⓐ forest fires are mostly smoke   Ⓑ trains are slower than flames   Ⓒ forest fires spread very rapidly   Ⓓ moving trains will not burn
7. **This train was stopped by**   Ⓐ people leaving the town   Ⓑ thick smoke   Ⓒ flames from the fire   Ⓓ dry woods
8. **When the people stopped the train**   Ⓐ they could not get on   Ⓑ they were burning   Ⓒ it ran over them   Ⓓ the conductor helped them on

No. right	1	2	3	4	5	6	7	8
G score	2.6	3.2	3.7	4.3	4.9	5.6	6.4	7.2

The blue jay is a brave, busy bird. Long after the songbirds have flown to the sunny south, you may see jays dodging among the bare trees. Even on very cold days when everything is covered with snow, if you go far into the woods, it is likely that you will see a company of jays braving the storm. They are so busy looking for food that they have no time to think about the cold. Now and then they find a dried berry or a nut that has fallen in some sheltered spot where the snow has not covered it. Sometimes they eat the tiny eggs of some insect hidden on the under side of a rough piece of bark. Even better, blue jays like the seeds that people put into the bird feeders in their yards during the winter.

9

1. **One of the northern winter birds is the**   Ⓐ bluebird   Ⓑ oriole   Ⓒ swallow   Ⓓ blue jay
2. **The blue jay eats**   Ⓐ crickets   Ⓑ bark   Ⓒ dried berries   Ⓓ grass
3. **In the winter many birds fly**   Ⓐ east   Ⓑ west   Ⓒ north   Ⓓ south
4. **The blue jay is busy**   Ⓐ singing   Ⓑ trying to keep warm   Ⓒ hunting food   Ⓓ making friends
5. **The blue jay is**   Ⓐ brave   Ⓑ weak   Ⓒ lazy   Ⓓ sly
6. **Some insects hide their eggs**   Ⓐ under bark   Ⓑ in nests   Ⓒ on feeders   Ⓓ in the snow
7. **During a storm the jay goes**   Ⓐ near the river   Ⓑ into the woods   Ⓒ to the sunny south   Ⓓ to the mountains
8. **It is hard for the jay to find food when the ground is covered with**   Ⓐ snow   Ⓑ leaves   Ⓒ grass   Ⓓ dust

No. right	1	2	3	4	5	6	7	8
G score	2.3	2.6	3.4	4.0	4.8	5.7	6.7	7.6

10

Our winter is the pleasantest season of the year. There is no snow or ice. Days are warm and comfortable, but nights are chilly. All day long, happy birds fly about, and at night the nightingales sing their beautiful songs. Orange trees blossom in March, and some even bear their loads of fruit during January and February. In February the rose trees cover the sides of houses with masses of blossoms—red, pink, yellow, and other colors. Then, too, the magnolia trees are in full bloom and make the air heavy with their fragrance. On the lawns the grapefruit trees drop their ripened products, which look like balls of pure gold. This land of sunshine and song, of fruit, flowers, and fragrance, is Florida.

1. **Where does the writer live?** Ⓐ in the north Ⓑ in Florida Ⓒ in a cold country Ⓓ in a desert
2. **Winter days in this state are** Ⓐ cold Ⓑ hot Ⓒ chilly Ⓓ warm
3. **Orange trees are in blossom in** Ⓐ December Ⓑ March Ⓒ spring Ⓓ May
4. **The writer says roses are in bloom in** Ⓐ June Ⓑ daytime Ⓒ February Ⓓ summer
5. **Nightingales sing** Ⓐ at night Ⓑ at noon Ⓒ all day Ⓓ at sunset
6. **Magnolia trees are in full bloom in** Ⓐ December Ⓑ March Ⓒ July Ⓓ February
7. **Ripe grapefruit look** Ⓐ golden Ⓑ green Ⓒ red Ⓓ orange
8. **How does the author feel about Florida?** Ⓐ appreciative Ⓑ chilly Ⓒ bored Ⓓ unhappy

No. right	1	2	3	4	5	6	7	8
G score	2.7	3.3	3.8	4.3	4.9	5.6	6.2	7.0

Most ants are hard workers and often work from six o'clock in the morning until ten o'clock at night. The work is divided among the worker ants so that each one has a certain amount to do. We do not know how they decide what each one is to do, for they do not talk. Some people think ants follow each other by their sense of smell. Ants often live to be a year old, and some have been known to live six or seven years. One way they get their food is from plant lice, which we might call their cows. The ants milk these "cows" by tapping the lice gently until a drop of syrupy "milk" comes out. Then they drink it. Ants take very good care of these plant lice and often build a covering over them so that they will be protected from the rain.

11

1. **Most ants are**   Ⓐ busy   Ⓑ lazy   Ⓒ careless   Ⓓ slow
2. **How many hours do ants usually work at one time?**   Ⓐ few   Ⓑ one   Ⓒ several   Ⓓ many
3. **Each worker ant does**   Ⓐ some work   Ⓑ no work   Ⓒ whatever he likes   Ⓓ little work
4. **Some people think ants follow each other by their sense of**   Ⓐ sight   Ⓑ hearing   Ⓒ touch   Ⓓ smell
5. **What is the longest time that ants have been known to live?**   Ⓐ one year   Ⓑ five years   Ⓒ seven years   Ⓓ eight years
6. **What we call ant cows are really**   Ⓐ caterpillars   Ⓑ bees   Ⓒ lice   Ⓓ flies
7. **These ant cows give**   Ⓐ milk   Ⓑ water   Ⓒ sugar   Ⓓ a syrup
8. **Choose the best title:**   Ⓐ How Ants Help Lice   Ⓑ The Ants and Their "Cows"   Ⓒ How Ants Talk   Ⓓ Milking Cows

No. right	1	2	3	4	5	6	7	8
G score	2.0	2.4	3.0	3.8	4.7	5.8	6.9	8.0

12

It was the last half of the ninth inning. The score stood 2 to 1 in favor of the Yankees. The Dodgers, then the "beloved bums" of Brooklyn, were at bat. There were two out and two men on base. Bill Bevans of the Yankees was on the mound. A few more successful pitches and he would enter baseball's hall of fame for having pitched the first no-hitter in the history of the World Series.

Lavagetto, who had been longest with the Dodgers, was sent in as a pinch hitter. Rubbing dirt on his hands, this player, who was nearly a has-been, strode to the plate, struck viciously at the first pitch and missed. New York fans yelled for joy, and Brooklyn was in breathless suspense. Lavagetto swung again, connected, and the ball soared over the head of the farthest outfielder.

As the Dodgers did a victory dance, the Yankees' pitcher trudged off the field with bowed head and tears in his eyes.

1. This is a story about which sport?   Ⓐ tennis   Ⓑ golf   Ⓒ baseball   Ⓓ football
2. At the beginning of the last half of the ninth inning, the score was
   Ⓐ 2 to 1   Ⓑ 2 to 2   Ⓒ 3 to 1   Ⓓ 3 to 2
3. Who won this game?   Ⓐ Yankees   Ⓑ Bill Bevans   Ⓒ New York   Ⓓ Dodgers
4. The Yankees were   Ⓐ disappointed   Ⓑ disagreeable   Ⓒ triumphant   Ⓓ joyful
5. When the batter missed, the New York fans   Ⓐ yelled for joy   Ⓑ shed tears   Ⓒ bowed their heads   Ⓓ moaned
6. What did the victors do?   Ⓐ wept   Ⓑ danced   Ⓒ shouted   Ⓓ yelled for joy
7. When the game ended, who trudged sadly off the field?
   Ⓐ Bill Bevans   Ⓑ Lavagetto   Ⓒ an outfielder   Ⓓ a Dodger
8. Bevans' first pitch was a   Ⓐ failure   Ⓑ poor try   Ⓒ success   Ⓓ wild throw

No. right	1	2	3	4	5	6	7	8
G score	2.6	3.3	3.7	4.3	4.8	5.6	6.3	7.0

The people of Japan show their love for nature in many of their customs. When the first snow falls, all the stores are closed, and the people gather on the hills to admire the beauty of the earth in its white robe. Later, when the plum trees bloom, the people crowd about them in admiration. They often give wooden crutches to the tired trees whose branches are bowing down with age. When the cherry trees blossom with delicate white flowers, the people gather on the shore or pass in little boats under the bending boughs, giving thanks for the wonderful beauty. In autumn when the moon is very bright, people sleep in the daytime so they may stay awake at night to watch the moon.

13

1. **The people of Japan show their love for nature in their**   Ⓐ dress   Ⓑ customs   Ⓒ stores   Ⓓ hills
2. **The stores are closed**   Ⓐ when the plum trees bloom   Ⓑ when the cherry trees bloom   Ⓒ when the first snow falls   Ⓓ when the trees bow down with age
3. **The people give crutches to the**   Ⓐ old men   Ⓑ delicate flowers   Ⓒ people on the hills   Ⓓ tired trees
4. **The people gather on the hills to**   Ⓐ admire the beauty of the earth   Ⓑ pick flowers   Ⓒ cut down trees   Ⓓ keep the stores closed
5. **When the cherry trees bloom the people give thanks for the**   Ⓐ boats   Ⓑ stores   Ⓒ crutches   Ⓓ beauty
6. **In the autumn the moon is**   Ⓐ small   Ⓑ dark   Ⓒ dull   Ⓓ very bright
7. **They stay awake at night to**   Ⓐ see the cherry trees   Ⓑ ride in little boats   Ⓒ watch the moon   Ⓓ gather on the hills
8. **When the plum trees bloom, the people**   Ⓐ bow down   Ⓑ wear white robes   Ⓒ sleep   Ⓓ crowd about them

No. right	1	2	3	4	5	6	7	8
G score	2.4	2.7	3.5	4.2	5.1	6.0	7.0	8.0

14

Elizabeth went to the window where she sat down to wait for Rocky. Rocky was the name she had given to a raccoon who had come to their house every night for the past week. Each night he had gotten into the garbage and spread bits of paper and fruit peelings all over the yard, which angered Elizabeth's father. Rocky always came at night because, like the owl, the bat, and the mouse, the raccoon is a nocturnal animal. These animals wander about at night and sleep during the day.

That day her father had built a new fence around the garbage cans, and she wondered if Rocky would be able to get to them. She did not have to wait long to see. Very soon, Rocky scurried around the back of the house and went straight to the new fence and sniffed. Next he scratched at the wooden slats trying to climb up, but there was nothing for his curved toes to grab onto. Discouraged, he left, and Elizabeth wondered if she would ever see Rocky again. She probably would not. Because raccoons are shy of humans, Rocky did not come to make friends. He only wanted food, and since he could no longer get to it, he would not return.

1. **The raccoon came looking for**   Ⓐ Elizabeth   Ⓑ food   Ⓒ mice   Ⓓ humans
2. **Elizabeth's father was angry because**   Ⓐ Rocky had scratched a hole in the screen   Ⓑ Rocky had kept Elizabeth up   Ⓒ Rocky had spread garbage all over the yard   Ⓓ Rocky had scared their pet poodle
3. **Like other creatures of the night, raccoons are**   Ⓐ nocturnal   Ⓑ centennial   Ⓒ diurnal   Ⓓ aquatic
4. **During the day, raccoons**   Ⓐ play   Ⓑ eat   Ⓒ explore   Ⓓ sleep
5. **To keep Rocky out of the garbage, Elizabeth's father**   Ⓐ built a fence around the yard   Ⓑ got a dog to scare him away   Ⓒ banged on a garbage can to frighten him   Ⓓ built a fence around the garbage cans
6. **Rocky tried to climb the fence**   Ⓐ and succeeded   Ⓑ but couldn't get hold of the chicken wire   Ⓒ but couldn't get a hold on the wooden slats   Ⓓ and took the tops off the garbage cans
7. **The raccoon would not come back because he**   Ⓐ was angry   Ⓑ was afraid   Ⓒ only wanted the food   Ⓓ went looking for a friend
8. **Rocky would not make friends with Elizabeth because**   Ⓐ he did not like the name Rocky   Ⓑ he liked someone else better   Ⓒ raccoons only like bats   Ⓓ raccoons are afraid of humans

No. right	1	2	3	4	5	6	7	8
G score	3.0	3.5	3.9	4.5	5.1	5.7	6.4	7.1

Many people know about Paul Revere's famous midnight ride. What many do not know is that a sixteen-year-old girl, Sybil Ludington, also rode on horseback through the night to warn her neighbors that the British were burning Danbury, Connecticut.

Sybil's father was an American army officer, and she rode forty miles to call out the men of his regiment. Four hundred of them responded.

Two hundred years later, an 8¢ postage stamp was issued to honor her, and a special television program was made about her brave deed.

15

1. **How old was Sybil when she made her ride?**   Ⓐ eight   Ⓑ sixteen   Ⓒ forty   Ⓓ twenty-six
2. **Sybil's father was**   Ⓐ Paul Revere   Ⓑ British   Ⓒ a television executive   Ⓓ in the army
3. **She rode**   Ⓐ 16 miles   Ⓑ 400 miles   Ⓒ 200 miles   Ⓓ 40 miles
4. **Danbury was burned by**   Ⓐ the British   Ⓑ Paul Revere   Ⓒ 400 men   Ⓓ her neighbors
5. **The men who answered Sybil's call for help were all**   Ⓐ living in Danbury   Ⓑ in her father's regiment   Ⓒ British   Ⓓ famous
6. **Sybil was honored with a**   Ⓐ statue   Ⓑ stamp   Ⓒ star   Ⓓ coin
7. **A television program was made about**   Ⓐ Danbury   Ⓑ Sybil Ludington   Ⓒ Connecticut   Ⓓ Colonel Ludington
8. **Sybil was *not* one of these:**   Ⓐ courageous   Ⓑ a good horseback rider   Ⓒ a heroine   Ⓓ a TV actress

No. right	1	2	3	4	5	6	7	8
G score	2.6	3.2	3.7	4.4	5.3	6.1	7.0	7.9

16

This true story was in many newspapers. A cat walked home a distance of 250 miles. Tiger, the cat, was lost in Wausau, Wisconsin, in June when his owners, Tim and Susan, were on their summer vacation. The following February, Tiger reached his home in Dubuque, Iowa. He made it on his own four paws.

Tiger was in good health and had even gotten a little fat. His happy family had only one question: How did he cross the Mississippi river? Tiger is keeping it a secret.

1. **Tiger walked**   Ⓐ from Iowa to Wisconsin   Ⓑ from the Mississippi River to Wausau   Ⓒ from Wisconsin to Iowa   Ⓓ from Dubuque to Mississippi
2. **Tiger's owners**   Ⓐ lost him   Ⓑ gave him away   Ⓒ sent him on vacation   Ⓓ left him home
3. **Tiger's journey took him**   Ⓐ a year   Ⓑ five weeks   Ⓒ eight months   Ⓓ eight days
4. **When Tiger reached home, he was**   Ⓐ skinny   Ⓑ sick   Ⓒ healthy   Ⓓ unhappy
5. **The cat had traveled**   Ⓐ 250 miles   Ⓑ 520 miles   Ⓒ 502 miles   Ⓓ 205 miles
6. **He crossed the**   Ⓐ Ohio River   Ⓑ Hudson River   Ⓒ Missouri River   Ⓓ Mississippi River
7. **When he came home, his owners were**   Ⓐ lonely   Ⓑ a little fat   Ⓒ joyful   Ⓓ on vacation
8. **The way Tiger crossed the river was**   Ⓐ by boat   Ⓑ by bridge   Ⓒ by swimming   Ⓓ unknown

No. right	1	2	3	4	5	6	7	8
G score	2.2	2.6	3.3	4.1	5.0	6.0	7.1	8.3

Our winters are very long and cold. The first frost of the season usually comes about the middle of August. Soon the leaves on the maple and oak trees on the hillsides turn red, yellow, and brown, forming a mass of color too beautiful to describe. Gradually the leaves fall from all the trees except the evergreens. The earliest snowfall in the Green Mountains usually comes in October. Before Christmas, deep snow sometimes covers the fields and mountains. Then I have fun. I coast on my long sled down the steep hills or go on my skis. After a heavy snowfall, I go for long hikes on my snowshoes. Sometimes it is very cold. I remember when it was fifty-six degrees below zero. The old people said that was uncommonly cold even for our part of the country. All winter the ponds and streams lie under their roofs of ice while I skate on them. Late in March the snow begins to melt, the ice breaks, and our long winter gives place to spring.

1. **Where does this author live?**   Ⓐ in the south   Ⓑ in the north   Ⓒ in Augusta   Ⓓ in a warm country
2. **Winters there are very**   Ⓐ short   Ⓑ warm   Ⓒ mild   Ⓓ long
3. **The first frost comes in**   Ⓐ March   Ⓑ October   Ⓒ August   Ⓓ December
4. **The leaves in the autumn are**   Ⓐ green   Ⓑ white   Ⓒ new   Ⓓ red and yellow
5. **The only trees that keep their color all winter are the**   Ⓐ evergreens   Ⓑ maple   Ⓒ oak   Ⓓ apple
6. **The first snow falls in**   Ⓐ December   Ⓑ October   Ⓒ March   Ⓓ August
7. **The snow begins to melt in**   Ⓐ March   Ⓑ February   Ⓒ August   Ⓓ April
8. **The writer**   Ⓐ enjoys winter sports   Ⓑ is fifty-six   Ⓒ breaks the ice   Ⓓ lives far from the mountains

No. right	1	2	3	4	5	6	7	8
G score	3.3	3.7	4.3	4.9	5.6	6.3	7.1	7.8

18

When bombs began falling more and more frequently on the crowded cities of England during World War II, the safety of their children became the chief concern of English parents.

Trains were needed to transport soldiers, but for several days these trains were put to a different use. The children had to be cared for first, and so they left their homes and parents and boarded trains, carrying suitcases and knapsacks. As soon as one train was full, it pulled out, and another train came in. Thousands of trains loaded with children streamed from the cities to homes in the country. England was at war, and the young generation had to be preserved.

Mothers went with their babies but not with children of school age. A tag giving name, address, and school in the big city was fastened to the coat of each of the older children. Most of them went to homes they had never seen before to live with persons they did not know.

1. **This evacuation of children took place in**   Ⓐ Ireland   Ⓑ Glasgow   Ⓒ Scotland   Ⓓ England
2. **The most important people in this story were the**   Ⓐ soldiers   Ⓑ mothers   Ⓒ children   Ⓓ workers
3. **How many children left their homes?**   Ⓐ hundreds   Ⓑ a thousand   Ⓒ many thousands   Ⓓ dozens
4. **The children were evacuated in order to**   Ⓐ save their lives   Ⓑ work in factories   Ⓒ attend a circus   Ⓓ visit relatives
5. **Mothers went with the**   Ⓐ older children   Ⓑ soldiers   Ⓒ babies   Ⓓ fathers
6. **The children were taken to**   Ⓐ other large cities   Ⓑ the country   Ⓒ London   Ⓓ a picnic
7. **Fastened to the coat of each child was**   Ⓐ a national flag   Ⓑ a flower   Ⓒ a beautiful badge   Ⓓ an identification tag
8. **Most of the children went to live with**   Ⓐ strangers   Ⓑ cousins   Ⓒ grandparents   Ⓓ old friends

No. right	1	2	3	4	5	6	7	8
G score	3.3	3.7	4.2	4.7	5.4	6.0	6.7	7.4

When I was a girl, I lived near the edge of a lake. I fished in it, partly because it was fun and partly because we needed the fish for food. But often I was too busy to sit by the water and wait for the fish to bite. After much thought, I worked out a plan to work and fish at the same time. I hung a small bell in the window of our house and ran a string from the bell down to my line at the water's edge. When a fish caught my hook, it would pull the string and ring the bell.

Recently I read there is a spider that fastens a thread to his web and then carries the thread to a hole where he hides and sleeps. When an insect flies into the web, the jerking of the thread tells the spider that food is waiting for him. The awakened spider runs down the thread to get the insect. So you see my plan was not very original after all!

1. **Which word best describes the writer?** Ⓐ inventive Ⓑ selfish Ⓒ lazy Ⓓ disgusted
2. **The writer could not wait for the fish because she was too** Ⓐ young Ⓑ busy Ⓒ hungry Ⓓ sleepy
3. **The fish gave us** Ⓐ food Ⓑ water Ⓒ work Ⓓ rest
4. **A bell hung** Ⓐ near the lake Ⓑ on the fish pole Ⓒ in the window Ⓓ in my kitchen
5. **A string ran from the bell to** Ⓐ my fishing rod Ⓑ the window Ⓒ my boat Ⓓ my line
6. **The spider used his thread** Ⓐ for tying the insect Ⓑ for swinging Ⓒ as a signal cord Ⓓ to catch a fish
7. **The spider's thread runs from his web to** Ⓐ the insect Ⓑ his hole Ⓒ the ground Ⓓ a nest
8. **My plan and the spider's saved** Ⓐ food Ⓑ money Ⓒ time Ⓓ rest

No. right	1	2	3	4	5	6	7	8
G score	3.5	3.9	4.4	5.0	5.6	6.1	6.8	7.4

20

The first day in Paris, Jaime's family decided to see the Eiffel Tower. It was built from 7000 tons of iron by an engineer, Alexandre Eiffel, for the World's Fair of 1889. Jaime's family decided to go as high up as they could. That meant going to the third level, 906 feet up. They would have to change elevators to go that far.

It was so windy and high they felt like they were going to fall off. Since there were high fences around the observation platform they wouldn't, but they still felt safer holding each other's hand.

Nothing they could see was as high as they were except perhaps one skyscraper far in the distance. Everything else looked miniature. They could see speedboats racing far below them on the Seine River. Happy and windblown they boarded the huge elevator for the trip down to earth.

1. **The Eiffel Tower was built**   Ⓐ as a war memorial   Ⓑ as a weather tower   Ⓒ as an exhibit for the World's Fair   Ⓓ as a radio tower
2. **People go to the top of the Eiffel Tower to see**   Ⓐ the elevators   Ⓑ the view   Ⓒ a skyscraper   Ⓓ miniatures
3. **The family got to the top of the tower by**   Ⓐ walking up the steps   Ⓑ a moving staircase   Ⓒ a helicopter   Ⓓ an elevator
4. **The highest level to which visitors can go on the tower is**   Ⓐ 3rd level   Ⓑ 13th floor   Ⓒ 5th level   Ⓓ 4th floor
5. **At the top of the tower the family**   Ⓐ could see many tall buildings   Ⓑ could see all of Paris   Ⓒ couldn't see well because of the fog   Ⓓ met Alexandre Eiffel
6. **The river that runs below the Eiffel Tower is the**   Ⓐ Amazon   Ⓑ Mississippi   Ⓒ Nile   Ⓓ Seine
7. **The tower is made of**   Ⓐ 600 tons of aluminum   Ⓑ 7000 tons of iron   Ⓒ 600 tons of steel   Ⓓ 600 tons of iron
8. **Which words best describe what it is like at the top of the Eiffel Tower?**   Ⓐ dangerous and scary   Ⓑ windy and spectacular   Ⓒ boring and confining   Ⓓ tiring and dizzying

No. right	1	2	3	4	5	6	7	8
G score	3.3	3.7	4.2	4.7	5.4	6.0	6.8	7.4

The people on Jane Street in New York City have planted a garden in a small vacant lot. About forty or fifty people of all ages worked on the garden at various times. Everyone is welcome to come in and enjoy it whenever the gate is open.

Twenty-two five-year-olds visited the garden with their teacher. They explored the herb garden in the center and were shown how to smell mint, spearmint, sage, chamomile, strawberries, and other fragrances. The children were especially enchanted by the Halloween witch scarecrow that the Jane Street neighbors had made.

People give presents to the garden. Someone left two statues outside the fence. Sometimes people throw out good things, and once a sculpture of a woman was fished out of a garbage can. She now stands near a wall in the beautiful, friendly garden where everyone can admire her, the flowers, and the trees.

1. **The garden was made by** Ⓐ 22 children Ⓑ New York City Ⓒ neighbors on Jane Street Ⓓ teachers
2. **The garden is** Ⓐ on what was a small, empty piece of land Ⓑ outside a fence Ⓒ next to a herb garden Ⓓ enchanted
3. **The people who worked on the garden were** Ⓐ twenty-two years old Ⓑ children Ⓒ all ages Ⓓ forty or fifty years old
4. **The children were shown plants that** Ⓐ were scented Ⓑ blossomed Ⓒ grow on trees Ⓓ had berries
5. **How did the garden get two of its statues?** Ⓐ people bought them Ⓑ children made them for Halloween Ⓒ they were given as gifts Ⓓ they were thrown over the fence
6. **One statue was found** Ⓐ near a wall Ⓑ in a garbage can Ⓒ in a herb garden Ⓓ by the gate
7. **The statue near the wall is of** Ⓐ a witch Ⓑ a woman Ⓒ a scarecrow Ⓓ a neighbor
8. **The garden is enjoyed by** Ⓐ the people on Jane Street Ⓑ 40 or 50 people Ⓒ children who like strawberries and spearmint Ⓓ everyone

No. right	1	2	3	4	5	6	7	8
G score	4.2	4.6	5.1	5.5	6.0	6.5	7.0	7.4

22

Careful parents take their children to a doctor for vaccinations. The vaccines immunize them against many dangerous diseases.

Adults remember a time when there was no vaccination for polio. Though many polio victims fully recovered, some died, and many others became crippled. Parents were relieved when Dr. Jonas Salk developed his famous vaccine.

Even today some children are in danger of contracting polio. These are the children who have never received the polio vaccine. Other diseases controlled by vaccines are measles, mumps, rubella, diptheria, and whooping cough. Lucky is the child who is protected against them all.

1. **Measles and mumps are** Ⓐ careful parents Ⓑ vaccinations Ⓒ doctors Ⓓ diseases
2. **Dr. Jonas Salk developed** Ⓐ polio Ⓑ a vaccine Ⓒ measles Ⓓ many dangerous diseases
3. **To immunize means** Ⓐ to contract Ⓑ to become crippled Ⓒ to protect Ⓓ to be sick
4. **Among children who had polio** Ⓐ some died Ⓑ none died Ⓒ all died Ⓓ all recovered
5. **When Dr. Salk developed his vaccine, parents were** Ⓐ thankful Ⓑ disappointed Ⓒ sick with polio Ⓓ in danger
6. **The disease that cripples is** Ⓐ measles Ⓑ mumps Ⓒ whooping cough Ⓓ polio
7. **A good title for this selection would be** Ⓐ All About Measles Ⓑ Preventing Dangerous Diseases Ⓒ Dr. Jonas Salk Ⓓ Children Who Died
8. **Lucky children** Ⓐ have had polio Ⓑ have not received any vaccinations Ⓒ have had their vaccinations Ⓓ will get the measles

No. right	1	2	3	4	5	6	7	8
G score	3.3	3.7	4.2	4.7	5.3	6.0	6.7	7.3

People all over the world enjoy dancing. Young and old, male and female, like to dance and to watch others dance. Did you ever wonder why dancing is so popular or how it began?

People often motion with their hands while talking. These gestures help express their feelings. Movement is a form of communication, and through movement people express themselves.

History shows that people have always danced. The people of ancient Greece and Egypt danced to honor their gods. All cultures at some time have had dances to bring rain, good health, or to chase evil spirits away. Dance, as we know it today, developed from these rituals. Many kinds of dancing, including ballet, ballroom dancing, and even disco steps, are often a way of expressing some inner feelings. In some ways dancing can express these feelings much better than words. Maybe that is why people all over the world enjoy dancing.

23

1. **Dancing is enjoyed by** Ⓐ mostly younger people Ⓑ mostly older people Ⓒ younger women Ⓓ young and old, male and female
2. **The point of the story is that dancing is** Ⓐ mostly done in the theatre Ⓑ a very difficult art Ⓒ a popular form of communication Ⓓ a kind of religion
3. **History shows that people danced** Ⓐ only in Egypt and Greece Ⓑ only to ask for rain Ⓒ only for enjoyment Ⓓ throughout the ages
4. **This story says that disco dancing is** Ⓐ a waste of time Ⓑ meaningless fun Ⓒ often a way of expressing inner feelings Ⓓ not as important as ballet
5. **Choose the best title:** Ⓐ Why Dancing Is So Popular Ⓑ The Religions of Greece and Egypt Ⓒ Learning to Dance Ⓓ Improving Your Health
6. **The story says that people move their hands while talking because they need to** Ⓐ attract attention Ⓑ express feelings Ⓒ exercise their arms Ⓓ chase away evil spirits
7. **Dance, as we know it today, developed from** Ⓐ ancient rituals Ⓑ early American customs Ⓒ talking Ⓓ the theatre
8. **The story says that many people enjoy dancing because it** Ⓐ keeps away evil spirits Ⓑ costs very little money Ⓒ can sometimes express feelings much better than words Ⓓ is very difficult to learn

No. right	1	2	3	4	5	6	7	8
G score	2.5	3.2	3.8	4.6	5.4	6.3	7.2	8.2

24

Peter was spending a very special summer day at the beach with his father. They started with a brisk swim in the morning, since it was high tide and the water was deep enough for swimming. Then they began work on a sand castle with tunnels and moats and stairs leading to the high tower. When they had finished their work, they stood back to admire the castle. It was indeed a work of art.

All the time Peter and his father were working on the sand castle, the tide had been going out, leaving a world of tidal pools for them to investigate. After lunch they went from one shallow pool to another, collecting snails and fiddler crabs and shiny rocks. They even found the skeleton of a horseshoe crab. Peter's father explained that horseshoe crabs are one of the oldest living creatures, dating back to the days of the dinosaurs.

By mid-afternoon Peter noticed that the tidal pools were filling back up again as the tide started to come in. They gathered their sea treasures and brought them back to shore. Then the tide was high again, and they went for another swim before setting off for home.

1. **Peter knew that it was high tide because**   Ⓐ the water was deep enough to go swimming   Ⓑ there was a red flag up   Ⓒ the wind was blowing toward the south   Ⓓ the shells left on the beach were still wet
2. **A sand castle is**   Ⓐ a game of cards for two players   Ⓑ a game played with buckets at the beach   Ⓒ buildings, moats, and towers made of sand   Ⓓ a place to store sand
3. **When the tide went out, Peter and his father investigated**   Ⓐ the seashells left on the beach   Ⓑ the sandbars out by the channel   Ⓒ the horseshoe crabs in the seaweed   Ⓓ the tidal pools
4. **A tidal pool is**   Ⓐ a swimming pool   Ⓑ a body of deep water between two sandbars   Ⓒ a shallow pool left by the out-going tide   Ⓓ a shallow pool dug by a horseshoe crab
5. **One of the oldest living creatures still found at the seashore is the**   Ⓐ horseshoe crab   Ⓑ hermit crab   Ⓒ fiddler crab   Ⓓ blue crab
6. **Peter knew that the tide was coming back in again because**   Ⓐ the people on the beach went home   Ⓑ the boats came back to port   Ⓒ the tidal pools started to fill back up with water   Ⓓ the seagulls flew away
7. **The last thing they did that day on the beach was**   Ⓐ fill the pools   Ⓑ find treasure   Ⓒ swim   Ⓓ build a castle
8. **Peter learned a lot about**   Ⓐ plants   Ⓑ marine life   Ⓒ rocks   Ⓓ swimming

No. right	1	2	3	4	5	6	7	8
G score	2.6	3.3	3.8	4.6	5.4	6.3	7.2	8.2

Did you know a tree could own land? In Georgia there is an old, old oak tree. Its owner loved this sturdy oak so much that he deeded to the tree the land on which it stood. He did this because he wished the tree always to be protected. It is many years since the man, Mr. Jackson, made this tree a land owner. Since then a few other trees have received gifts of the land on which they grow. You might say that old trees are citizens that everyone looks up to!

1. **This story tells how a tree happened to** Ⓐ grow Ⓑ own land Ⓒ be cut down Ⓓ be loved
2. **The name of the tree's owner was** Ⓐ Georgia Ⓑ Johnson Ⓒ Jackson Ⓓ Oak
3. **Mr. Jackson deeded the land to the tree** Ⓐ a year ago Ⓑ a short time ago Ⓒ a few years ago Ⓓ many years ago
4. **He wished the tree to be protected because** Ⓐ it was sturdy Ⓑ he loved it Ⓒ it was old Ⓓ it was an oak
5. **Mr. Jackson lived in** Ⓐ the city Ⓑ Oakland Ⓒ the country Ⓓ Georgia
6. **Deeding land to a tree** Ⓐ makes it grow Ⓑ keeps it strong Ⓒ makes it loved Ⓓ protects it
7. **What is the point of this story?** Ⓐ oak trees grow old Ⓑ things may own property Ⓒ many people love trees Ⓓ trees sign deeds
8. **Mr. Jackson was** Ⓐ a nature lover Ⓑ sturdy Ⓒ protected Ⓓ a man who got gifts

No. right	1	2	3	4	5	6	7	8
G score	2.6	3.4	3.9	4.7	5.6	6.5	7.4	8.4

26

There is a game that never ends and never grows dull. Call it Exploring Your Own Questions. Perhaps your teacher will play it with you. Each of you must bring a question which you cannot answer but would *like to have answered*. It may be a question that has never been answered. Now, or in later years, you may make the world better by finding the answer. Edison answered his own question when he found out how to turn electricity into light.

The question you bring to school may be answered by some pupil or teacher, some adult in the community, some book, or some person to whom you write. Several of you may wish to search for the answer to the same question. You may well spend much of your time in school finding, or learning to find, the answers to your *own* questions.

1. **This game is called** Ⓐ Your Questions   Ⓑ Homemade Questions Ⓒ Parents' Questions   Ⓓ Exploring Your Own Questions
2. **Which question did Edison answer?**   Ⓐ how to use books   Ⓑ how to make the electric light   Ⓒ which adults in the community could help   Ⓓ his teacher's question about the world
3. **Who should think most about the answer to your question?**   Ⓐ you   Ⓑ your parents   Ⓒ your classmates   Ⓓ your teacher
4. **It is suggested that an answer to your question might result in**   Ⓐ world gain   Ⓑ personal success   Ⓒ class advancement   Ⓓ assistance to your teacher
5. **In searching for answers, this lesson says you may well use**   Ⓐ several hours   Ⓑ most of your homework time   Ⓒ much of your school time   Ⓓ vacation time
6. **The lesson says your question may be answered**   Ⓐ never   Ⓑ in later years   Ⓒ next week   Ⓓ tomorrow
7. **What kind of answer should there be to the question?**   Ⓐ one found quickly   Ⓑ a trivial one   Ⓒ an indifferent one   Ⓓ a worthwhile one
8. **To explore a question, you must**   Ⓐ buy books   Ⓑ ask an adult   Ⓒ work with another pupil   Ⓓ do research

No. right	1	2	3	4	5	6	7	8
G score	3.3	3.7	4.3	4.9	5.6	6.3	7.1	7.8

The highest point in the eastern United States is Clingman's Dome in Tennessee, about ten miles from New Found Gap. The Cherokee Indians claim there is an invisible lake called Atagahi between the Gap and the Dome. At night Cherokees on top of the Smoky Mountains claim they can hear the lake's waves lapping against the shores and the whirr of bird wings flying to the lake.

According to Cherokee legend, the lake exists to heal wounded animals and birds. By dipping into the water of Atagahi, ill animals and birds are cured and made whole again. Anyone who fasts seven days and nights is permitted to see the tracks of animals and birds on the lake's shore and to watch them coming to be healed.

27

1. **A legend is a**   Ⓐ fairy tale   Ⓑ fact   Ⓒ folktale   Ⓓ movie
2. **Atagahi is a**   Ⓐ lake   Ⓑ Indian   Ⓒ mountain   Ⓓ dome
3. **Invisible means**   Ⓐ a high point   Ⓑ can't be seen   Ⓒ Cherokee   Ⓓ healing
4. **The Indians say they can hear**   Ⓐ bird cries   Ⓑ animals   Ⓒ waves   Ⓓ storms
5. **Atagahi is believed to be**   Ⓐ ten miles from Tennessee   Ⓑ between the Gap and the Dome   Ⓒ on the top of Clingman's Dome   Ⓓ at the highest point in the eastern United States
6. **In order to see the tracks, the Cherokees say you must**   Ⓐ be religious   Ⓑ go without food for a week   Ⓒ climb to New Found Gap   Ⓓ be fast
7. **Animals and birds are said to go to the lake**   Ⓐ to be healed   Ⓑ to swim   Ⓒ to drink   Ⓓ to make tracks
8. **Choose the best title:**   Ⓐ A Cherokee Legend   Ⓑ Invisible Birds and Animals   Ⓒ New Found Lake   Ⓓ A Dip in the Lake

No. right	1	2	3	4	5	6	7	8
G score	3.5	3.9	4.6	5.2	5.9	6.7	7.4	8.3

28

Every June the people of Hameln remember one of history's great crimes. About 700 years ago, every single child in that German village was kidnapped.

At that time Hameln had a lot of rats. One day a traveler, who was passing through offered to get rid of them if he was paid. After the village agreed, the traveler started to play some sort of flute or oboe. The rats crawled out of houses and barns and followed the traveler to the nearby River Waser. There all the rats drowned. Then the village refused to pay. The traveler became very angry and left.

On June 26, 1284, the traveler returned and played his music again. 130 children followed him out the village's gate. One boy who had forgotten his coat returned. Another, who was blind, got lost and also returned. Later a third returned. Unfortunately, he was unable to speak. What happened to the rest of the children and to the traveler is still a mystery.

1. **How many children were kidnapped?** Ⓐ 700   Ⓑ every child in the village   Ⓒ 26   Ⓓ 127
2. **The traveler offered to get rid of the rats if the village**   Ⓐ would let him go home   Ⓑ would let him play music   Ⓒ paid him   Ⓓ would let him live near the river
3. **What happened to the rats?**   Ⓐ they drowned   Ⓑ the traveler poisoned them   Ⓒ they disappeared   Ⓓ the traveler led them to another village
4. **The traveler probably kidnapped the children because**   Ⓐ they laughed at him   Ⓑ a boy stole his flute   Ⓒ the village tried to put him in jail   Ⓓ the village broke its promise
5. **How many children disappeared forever?**   Ⓐ all of them   Ⓑ 130   Ⓒ 127   Ⓓ 26
6. **What happened to the traveler?**   Ⓐ he was caught   Ⓑ he later kidnapped the children of another village   Ⓒ he disappeared   Ⓓ he drowned
7. **The crime happened about**   Ⓐ 700 years ago   Ⓑ 1200 years ago   Ⓒ 200 years ago   Ⓓ 1784
8. **The last child to return**   Ⓐ was blind   Ⓑ couldn't speak   Ⓒ had forgotten his coat   Ⓓ had gotten lost

No. right	1	2	3	4	5	6	7	8
G score	2.8	3.5	4.0	4.7	5.6	6.5	7.4	8.4

You may have dreamed at some time of a land where everything was strange, where the animals did things that you read of in fairy tales, and where the trees and birds forgot the time of year. Should you travel, you could find a real topsy-turvy land in a jungle on a peninsula in Asia.

In this jungle there are no marked seasons. In one tree you may find birds nesting, and in the next tree birds of the same kind shedding their feathers; or you will see one tree with ripe fruit and a neighboring tree of the same kind beginning to blossom.

There are butterflies more than a foot wide. One small bird sleeps upside down. The male of another kind of bird sits on the eggs while his wife fights his battles for him. Fish hop, skip, and jump on the ground, and then climb trees. Later they may be seen walking down the trees to take a bath in a convenient pool. Crabs eat coconut, fish eat living coral, and rats live in the tops of tall trees.

Truly the Malay jungle is a topsy-turvy wonderland.

---

1. **The selection states that** Ⓐ rats fly Ⓑ fish hop Ⓒ crabs live forever Ⓓ trees shed feathers
2. **This story is primarily about** Ⓐ animals Ⓑ rivers Ⓒ travelers Ⓓ the fall season
3. **Some butterflies** Ⓐ eat living coral Ⓑ jump on the ground Ⓒ are more than 12 inches wide Ⓓ sit on their eggs
4. **The expression "no marked seasons" means** Ⓐ little difference between winter and summer Ⓑ people there have no calendar Ⓒ summer comes early Ⓓ there is no month of April
5. **This story is a** Ⓐ fairy tale Ⓑ dream Ⓒ true story Ⓓ fable
6. **The words "sleeps upside down" refer to a** Ⓐ rat Ⓑ fish Ⓒ bird Ⓓ snake
7. **A trip to the Malay jungle would be** Ⓐ convenient Ⓑ an unusual experience Ⓒ a fairy tale Ⓓ impossible in season
8. **Choose the best title:** Ⓐ An Asian Wonderland Ⓑ Fish Who Climb Trees Ⓒ A Peninsula Ⓓ Strange Birds and Trees

No. right	1	2	3	4	5	6	7	8
G score	3.4	3.8	4.5	5.2	5.9	6.7	7.4	8.4

30

The Chinese New Year takes place in late January or early February, and the celebration lasts fifteen days. Each year is named for one of twelve animals: boar, dog, rooster, monkey, ox, dragon, snake, horse, sheep, tiger, rabbit, or mouse.

People visit friends and relatives, usually bringing red paper envelopes with money inside for the children. Another usual gift is fruit. It is thought to be lucky to give and receive such presents.

There are parades to celebrate the new year. The parade is led by a big Golden Dragon, the Chinese symbol of strength.

1. **The Chinese New Year comes in** Ⓐ summer Ⓑ fall Ⓒ winter Ⓓ spring
2. **The celebration lasts** Ⓐ all of February Ⓑ twelve days Ⓒ two months Ⓓ two weeks and a day
3. **Each year is named for** Ⓐ an animal Ⓑ a friend Ⓒ a fruit Ⓓ a symbol of strength
4. **Which year is *never* celebrated by the Chinese?** Ⓐ The Year of the Tiger Ⓑ The Year of the Fox Ⓒ The Year of the Ox Ⓓ The Year of the Dog
5. **People give presents of** Ⓐ rabbits and sheep Ⓑ apples and grapes Ⓒ games and toys Ⓓ paper dragons
6. **The Chinese believe it is good luck to** Ⓐ give red envelopes with money in them Ⓑ go to a parade Ⓒ pick fruit Ⓓ get gifts that are made of paper
7. **The parade is led by** Ⓐ a Golden Rabbit Ⓑ a Golden Dragon Ⓒ a real dragon Ⓓ a red dragon
8. **To the Chinese, a dragon is something** Ⓐ unlucky Ⓑ silly Ⓒ strong Ⓓ simple

No. right	1	2	3	4	5	6	7	8
G score	**3.0**	**3.6**	**4.3**	**5.0**	**5.8**	**6.7**	**7.6**	**8.6**

An airplane pilot invited the skipper of a submarine to go up in a plane with him. The pilot scared the skipper by power diving close to the earth, looping the loop, and barrel rolling.

When the pilot was the skipper's guest, the skipper ordered the crew to take the submarine out to sea and then down as far as it could go without being crushed. The skipper and pilot watched the depth gauge. The pilot grew more and more frightened as the gauge crept toward the danger mark. Finally the skipper ordered the crew to bring the submarine up to the surface. But something went wrong. The submarine kept on going down. The skipper gave orders to his crew, but still the needle on the gauge read deeper and deeper. Suddenly the hatch of the submarine was thrown open and the pilot discovered that the submarine had never even left its pier.

1. **This lesson is the story of how two officers**   Ⓐ fought each other   Ⓑ became acquainted   Ⓒ played jokes on each other   Ⓓ angered each other
2. **The skipper was in charge of a**   Ⓐ plane   Ⓑ submarine   Ⓒ pier   Ⓓ pilot
3. **One of the pilot's tricks was**   Ⓐ gauge manipulation   Ⓑ racing   Ⓒ barrel rolling   Ⓓ shouting
4. **Why was the pilot able to do these stunts safely? He was**   Ⓐ a brave man   Ⓑ an expert pilot   Ⓒ an older man   Ⓓ an officer
5. **While in the airplane the skipper**   Ⓐ enjoyed himself   Ⓑ felt safe   Ⓒ was sick   Ⓓ was frightened
6. **The skipper played his trick by**   Ⓐ looping the loop   Ⓑ power diving   Ⓒ stunting   Ⓓ tampering with the gauge
7. **The crew of the submarine**   Ⓐ looped the loop   Ⓑ went toward danger   Ⓒ played their part   Ⓓ threw open the airplane hatch
8. **How did the skipper feel at the end?**   Ⓐ scared   Ⓑ that he had evened the score   Ⓒ relieved   Ⓓ that he made a discovery

No. right	1	2	3	4	5	6	7	8
G score	3.8	4.4	5.1	5.8	6.6	7.3	8.1	9.1

32

One of my animal friends was a water snake. On warm summer nights when rain was falling, he would leave the lake, crawl up the hill through the woods, and let the water from the roof of our house pour on him. Several rainy nights, when I turned on the outdoor light, I saw him with the rain water pouring down on his back.

One morning my wife called excitedly that a copperhead had run under the woodpile. I wanted no copperheads near the house so I poked him out with a stick. It wasn't a copperhead, but our water snake in a beautiful new skin.

When he started crawling down through the woods toward the lake, a catbird saw him. Since the catbird had a nest in one of the trees, she flew at the snake and gave his tail a sharp peck. The snake coiled and struck at the bird, but she hopped back up the hill about three feet. Hopping back and forth with wings outspread, the bird threatened to peck again. When she wouldn't get nearer, the snake uncoiled and started down the hill. Once more the bird flew in and gave a hard peck at her enemy's tail. Again the snake coiled and struck, but too late to catch the bird. This peck and coil was repeated until the snake reached the lake. He must have had a very sore tail.

1. **This story is mainly about a** Ⓐ copperhead Ⓑ water snake Ⓒ catbird Ⓓ wife
2. **The snake lives** Ⓐ in the lake Ⓑ under the woodpile Ⓒ by the house Ⓓ in the woods
3. **The snake comes to the house in** Ⓐ winter Ⓑ early spring Ⓒ summer Ⓓ late fall
4. **What did my wife think was under the woodpile? A** Ⓐ copperhead Ⓑ water snake Ⓒ catbird Ⓓ nest
5. **What part of the snake was pecked? The** Ⓐ head Ⓑ neck Ⓒ body Ⓓ tail
6. **What was in the tree?** Ⓐ a nest Ⓑ a snake Ⓒ a bird Ⓓ a copperhead
7. **Which was hurt most? The** Ⓐ snake Ⓑ wife Ⓒ nest Ⓓ bird
8. **Why did the bird peck the snake?** Ⓐ to protect the house Ⓑ she wanted to eat him Ⓒ she was afraid he would harm her babies Ⓓ to reach the lake

No. right	1	2	3	4	5	6	7	8
G score	3.2	3.7	4.3	5.1	5.9	6.8	7.6	8.7

When I was about ten years old, my mother was very ill. I wanted to give her a present of a pretty pink dress I had seen in a store window. The price of the dress was $2.40. I could buy the dress by picking 24 gallons of blackberries and selling them for ten cents a gallon.

There were blackberries near our house, but many persons picked there. I went up the mountain, following an old logging road, and found a deserted field. The briars were thick, and the berries were large and numerous. I soon filled a two-gallon bucket and followed the road back down the mountain. On my left was a huge oak tree, from which grew a sturdy limb stretching across the road. As I passed under it, I glanced up and saw something that just about scared me to death. A panther was stretched along the limb sound asleep. Since it was easier to go forward than backward, I tiptoed on bare feet on down the road. As I went, I turned my head to keep that panther in sight. Had it moved a muscle, I would have dropped the bucket of berries and galloped down the road faster than anything.

33

1. **The author wanted to give his mother a dress** Ⓐ for her birthday Ⓑ to make her feel better Ⓒ to wear to a party Ⓓ for Christmas
2. **He decided to get the money by** Ⓐ using his savings Ⓑ working in a store Ⓒ running errands Ⓓ picking and selling berries
3. **He picked berries** Ⓐ near the house Ⓑ near an oak tree Ⓒ up the mountain Ⓓ on a farm
4. **How did the panther respond?** Ⓐ he slept on Ⓑ he roared Ⓒ he yawned Ⓓ he ate the berries
5. **What did the boy do?** Ⓐ he galloped down the road Ⓑ he didn't move a muscle Ⓒ he went back to the field Ⓓ he tiptoed past the panther
6. **What happened to the bucket of berries?** Ⓐ he dropped it Ⓑ he ate them Ⓒ he probably got 20¢ for it Ⓓ the panther got it
7. **Why did the boy turn his head?** Ⓐ he was startled Ⓑ the panther woke up Ⓒ he heard a sound Ⓓ he wanted to make sure the panther remained asleep
8. **The author was** Ⓐ courageous Ⓑ a logger Ⓒ ill Ⓓ rich

No. right	1	2	3	4	5	6	7	8
G score	3.8	4.3	5.0	5.7	6.4	7.1	7.8	8.8

34

More than a hundred years ago there lived a little boy who could play wonderful music. At the age of nine he played before the great duke who ruled in his country.

One day at school his teacher was having a very hard time keeping the pupils quiet. He tried every way and was worn out. Then this boy went to the piano and began to play, telling a story about robbers. When he reached the part where they went to sleep in the forest, he played softly, oh so softly! After a while the room became very, very quiet. Suddenly the music ceased. The teacher, who had been listening with delight, glanced up. All the noisy, restless boys were asleep—every one of them. They were lulled to sleep by their classmate, Frederic Chopin, telling a story at the piano keyboard.

1. **About how long ago did this boy live?** Ⓐ fifty years Ⓑ many years Ⓒ one hundred years Ⓓ two hundred years
2. **Chopin was a** Ⓐ musician Ⓑ carpenter Ⓒ teacher Ⓓ duke
3. **At what age did he play for the ruler?** Ⓐ seven Ⓑ nine Ⓒ ten Ⓓ twenty
4. **The pupils were** Ⓐ joyful Ⓑ noisy Ⓒ angry Ⓓ girls
5. **The teacher tried to** Ⓐ punish them Ⓑ quiet them Ⓒ feed them Ⓓ put them to sleep
6. **The little boy went to the** Ⓐ piano Ⓑ organ Ⓒ harp Ⓓ radio
7. **He played** Ⓐ loudly Ⓑ slowly Ⓒ gayly Ⓓ softly
8. **The teacher was** Ⓐ angry Ⓑ startled Ⓒ delighted Ⓓ put to sleep

No. right	1	2	3	4	5	6	7	8
G score	3.2	3.7	4.4	5.1	5.9	6.8	7.6	8.6

Do not be careless like the thousands who drown each year.

Some of them get caught in the ocean's undertow, are carried out into deep water, and then become panicky. They should keep their heads, swim toward the shore each time a wave lifts them, and rest in the troughs of the waves.

Some get caught in a current and try to swim against it. They should swim with and across the current.

Some swim far from shore with no expert swimmer or boat near by.

Some plunge into cold water. They should wade in slowly. The shock of jumping into cold water when one is tired or hot may cause cramps, and cramps may cause drowning.

Some swim too soon after eating, and others swim until they are too cold. Either may cause cramps.

Some swim during a thunderstorm and are killed by lightning striking the water.

Some try to rescue others without using a boat, log, plank, rope, or other floating object. This is unwise for even expert swimmers to do.

35

---

1. **The story states that many lives are lost each year through**
   Ⓐ swimming   Ⓑ fear   Ⓒ fatigue   Ⓓ carelessness
2. **Swimmers are sometimes carried into deep water by**   Ⓐ troughs   Ⓑ undertow   Ⓒ cramps   Ⓓ extreme cold
3. **If caught in a current, a swimmer should try to swim**   Ⓐ against it   Ⓑ under it   Ⓒ with and across it   Ⓓ above and beyond it
4. **The safest way to enter cold water for a swim is to**   Ⓐ jump in   Ⓑ wade in   Ⓒ dive in   Ⓓ fall in
5. **After eating, it is safe to swim**   Ⓐ soon   Ⓑ immediately   Ⓒ after a rest   Ⓓ when one wishes
6. **Continuing to swim when one has become too cold may cause**
   Ⓐ hunger   Ⓑ fright   Ⓒ thirst   Ⓓ cramps
7. **When trying to rescue others in the water, one should use**   Ⓐ nothing   Ⓑ an undertow   Ⓒ some floating object   Ⓓ a short rope
8. **As a safety measure, everyone should learn to**   Ⓐ eat slowly   Ⓑ swim intelligently   Ⓒ dive into cold water   Ⓓ stay in the water during a storm

No. right	1	2	3	4	5	6	7	8
G score	3.8	4.3	5.0	5.7	6.4	7.1	7.8	8.8

36

A farmer had two geese—a gander and his mate. When an automobile killed the gander's mate, the farmer burned her in a large, heavy can. Since then, year after year, the gander has guarded the can, flapping his wings and pecking any animal or person who comes near it. He will have nothing to do with the other geese, except to fight them. Every spring, when the geese are hatching eggs, the farmer puts some tiny goslings in the can. He does this when the gander is asleep. When the farmer takes the goslings out of the can later, the gander, thinking they are his own, takes good care of them.

1. **This story is mainly about a**   Ⓐ goose that was killed   Ⓑ faithful gander   Ⓒ farmer   Ⓓ gosling
2. **What killed the goose?**   Ⓐ a car   Ⓑ the gander   Ⓒ the farmer   Ⓓ a can
3. **What did the farmer burn in the can? The**   Ⓐ gander   Ⓑ mate   Ⓒ goslings   Ⓓ goose eggs
4. **How long has the gander guarded the can?**   Ⓐ a day   Ⓑ a month   Ⓒ a year   Ⓓ several years
5. **The goose eggs are hatched in the**   Ⓐ spring   Ⓑ summer   Ⓒ autumn   Ⓓ winter
6. **The gander likes**   Ⓐ the farmer   Ⓑ the goslings   Ⓒ everyone   Ⓓ other geese
7. **What does the can have in it most of the time?**   Ⓐ nothing   Ⓑ the gander   Ⓒ the mate   Ⓓ goslings
8. **The gander takes good care of the**   Ⓐ farmer   Ⓑ other geese   Ⓒ goslings   Ⓓ automobile

No. right	1	2	3	4	5	6	7	8
G score	3.2	3.7	4.4	5.1	5.9	6.8	7.6	8.7

Chinese words are made up of many little marks instead of letters. These words are called characters. There is no alphabet, so children do not need to learn to spell. However, they have to learn at least 3,500 different characters before they can read a simple book. Hundreds of years ago, when the Chinese began to write, each word was a picture. The picture word for sun was a small circle with a dot in the middle, but it has since changed; now it is a small square with a line in the middle. The word for umbrella still looks like an open umbrella. Many words have been changed so much that they do not look like pictures today.

37

1. **When the Chinese began to write words, each one was a**   Ⓐ picture   Ⓑ letter   Ⓒ circle   Ⓓ dot
2. **Chinese words are called**   Ⓐ letters   Ⓑ marks   Ⓒ capitals   Ⓓ characters
3. **The word for umbrella looks like an umbrella that is**   Ⓐ small   Ⓑ broken   Ⓒ closed   Ⓓ open
4. **Chinese children have to learn**   Ⓐ 3,500 letters   Ⓑ to draw pictures   Ⓒ 3,500 characters   Ⓓ to spell 3,500 words
5. **Chinese people began to write**   Ⓐ hundreds of years ago   Ⓑ 3,500 years ago   Ⓒ in this century   Ⓓ instead of drawing
6. **A square with a line in the middle means**   Ⓐ sun   Ⓑ umbrella   Ⓒ China   Ⓓ picture
7. **If you went to school in China, you would have no**   Ⓐ arithmetic   Ⓑ reading   Ⓒ spelling   Ⓓ writing
8. **Choose the best title:**   Ⓐ The Chinese Sun   Ⓑ The Umbrella   Ⓒ Chinese Writing   Ⓓ The Chinese Alphabet

No. right	1	2	3	4	5	6	7	8
G score	2.5	3.2	3.8	4.6	5.6	6.6	7.6	8.8

38

Pretend you are going to write in Chinese. First get your ink stone, which is a small, flat, square piece of stone. Put a few drops of water on it. Take your ink out of your desk. It is not in a bottle. It is a small block of dry ink. Rub your block of ink in the water on the stone and you will have what looks like black paint. That is Chinese ink. You must have a brush pen to write with it.

Now pick up your sheet of paper. The lines on it run up and down the page instead of across it. Begin in the upper right-hand corner and write the words one under the other down the side of the page. When you have finished that column, begin another at the top of the page to the left of the first column. Chinese books are written this way too. If you should see a Chinese person open a book, you might think he or she was beginning at the back. It is not the back. It is the front in Chinese!

1. **On the stone put** Ⓐ some paint Ⓑ some water Ⓒ a bottle Ⓓ a pen
2. **At first the ink is** Ⓐ dry Ⓑ sticky Ⓒ damp Ⓓ wet
3. **You are to write with a** Ⓐ lead pencil Ⓑ brush Ⓒ fountain pen Ⓓ black crayon
4. **When ready to use, the ink looks like** Ⓐ soft clay Ⓑ paint Ⓒ water Ⓓ crayon
5. **Chinese is written** Ⓐ in columns Ⓑ from right to left Ⓒ down the left side first Ⓓ across the bottom of the page
6. **Write the words** Ⓐ one under the other Ⓑ side by side Ⓒ one above the other Ⓓ across the page
7. **Which of these is not needed to write in Chinese?** Ⓐ a brush Ⓑ paper Ⓒ a bottle of ink Ⓓ an ink stone
8. **You begin writing Chinese in the** Ⓐ upper left-hand corner Ⓑ lower right-hand corner Ⓒ upper right-hand corner Ⓓ lower left-hand corner

No. right	1	2	3	4	5	6	7	8
G score	3.3	3.8	4.5	5.2	6.0	6.9	7.6	8.7

Here is how a clever boy rescued a king's pearl out of a hole in a rock. First he collected some very fine sand which he placed in a little pile beside the hole. Next he found a long, slender bamboo twig that was dry and stiff. He put the bamboo twig down in the hole until it touched the pearl. Filling his left hand with sand, he poured a tiny trickle of it down into the hole, while, with the twig in his right hand, he stirred the pearl over and over and round and round. In this way the fine sand was stirred under the pearl, slowly lifting it until the boy could reach it with his fingers. When, with a bow, he returned the pearl to the king, laughter had given way to respect for the lad's cleverness.

39

1. **The twig the lad used was** Ⓐ wet Ⓑ short Ⓒ bamboo Ⓓ sandy
2. **What was the first thing that was done?** Ⓐ sand was collected Ⓑ the pearl was stirred Ⓒ the lad bowed Ⓓ the pearl was lifted
3. **Where was the sand first placed?** Ⓐ in the hole Ⓑ beside the hole Ⓒ under the pearl Ⓓ around the pearl
4. **His right hand** Ⓐ held the left hand Ⓑ held the sand Ⓒ poured the sand Ⓓ held the twig
5. **The sand was poured in** Ⓐ a pile Ⓑ very quickly Ⓒ very gradually Ⓓ with respect
6. **The pearl was returned to the** Ⓐ king Ⓑ boy Ⓒ hole Ⓓ sand
7. **What was the last thing the lad did?** Ⓐ got a twig Ⓑ returned the pearl Ⓒ laughed Ⓓ got some sand
8. **At the end, the king** Ⓐ laughed Ⓑ bowed Ⓒ gave the pearl to the boy Ⓓ admired the boy's intelligence.

No. right	1	2	3	4	5	6	7	8
G score	3.5	3.9	4.6	5.3	6.0	6.9	7.6	8.6

40

What is the tallest animal? A gorilla? An elephant? A giraffe, of course. Male giraffes grow to be eighteen feet tall. When a baby giraffe is born it is already about six feet tall. A grown giraffe usually has a neck about seven feet long. That's more than one third the length of his whole body. Nature has made the giraffe so tall so that it can find food in the high branches of trees.

Giraffes roam the African plains in small herds, led by a male. In spite of their awkward height, they are good at defending themselves. They can kill a lion with a kick from their hind hooves. They are most vulnerable when drinking because they have to bend down in such an awkward position. To help make up for this, nature has made them able to go without water for long periods of time. For some reason nature has made the giraffe unable to swim. It is one of the very few animals in the world that cannot swim at all.

1. **Giraffes can grow to be**   Ⓐ 7 ft. tall   Ⓑ 18 ft. tall   Ⓒ 25 ft. tall   Ⓓ 28 ft. tall
2. **They are tall so that they can**   Ⓐ kill lions   Ⓑ run fast   Ⓒ eat leaves in trees   Ⓓ go without water
3. **Giraffes are found**   Ⓐ all over the world   Ⓑ in India   Ⓒ in Africa   Ⓓ in Argentina
4. **Newborn giraffes are usually**   Ⓐ the size of babies   Ⓑ about 6 ft. tall   Ⓒ the size of full-grown giraffes   Ⓓ about 7 ft. tall
5. **Giraffes roam the plains**   Ⓐ in large herds   Ⓑ in small herds   Ⓒ alone   Ⓓ with a single mate
6. **Giraffes can kill a lion with**   Ⓐ a kick   Ⓑ a stick   Ⓒ a bite   Ⓓ their claws
7. **Vulnerable means**   Ⓐ good to drink   Ⓑ easy to attack   Ⓒ strongly defended   Ⓓ awkward
8. **Giraffes cannot**   Ⓐ drink   Ⓑ jump   Ⓒ run   Ⓓ swim

No. right	1	2	3	4	5	6	7	8
G score	3.0	3.7	4.3	5.1	5.9	6.8	7.6	8.7

Two travelers were on the road together when suddenly a bear appeared. One dashed to a tree at the side of the road, climbed up, and hid in its branches. The other was not as nimble and, as he could not escape, he threw himself on the ground and pretended to be dead. The bear came up and sniffed all around him, but he kept perfectly still and held his breath. Since bears do not like to touch a dead body, the trick worked, and the bear went away. When the coast was clear, the traveler in the tree came down and said, "I saw the bear put his mouth to your ear and whisper to you. What did he say?" The other replied, "He told me never again to travel with a friend who deserts you at the first sign of trouble."

1. **The bear**   Ⓐ climbed a tree   Ⓑ surprised the travelers   Ⓒ was not nimble   Ⓓ was traveling
2. **What did one traveler do?**   Ⓐ he ran away   Ⓑ he dashed to a tree and hid behind it   Ⓒ he threw himself on some branches   Ⓓ he climbed a tree
3. **The other person**   Ⓐ pretended to be a bear   Ⓑ could not run and climb   Ⓒ was a better athlete   Ⓓ was not afraid
4. **What did the second traveler do?**   Ⓐ he fell down dead   Ⓑ he escaped to the coast   Ⓒ he threw ground and branches at the bear   Ⓓ he lay down and didn't breath
5. **What did the bear do to the traveler?**   Ⓐ he whispered to him   Ⓑ he sniffed him   Ⓒ he killed him   Ⓓ he tricked him
6. **The bear went away because**   Ⓐ he didn't like to eat anything already dead   Ⓑ the man whispered a secret to him   Ⓒ he sniffed the man on the ground   Ⓓ he was afraid of being dead
7. **Why did the traveler come down from the tree?**   Ⓐ there was a dead body   Ⓑ to help his friend   Ⓒ to chase the bear   Ⓓ the danger was over
8. **A real friend**   Ⓐ will give you dessert   Ⓑ will tell you secrets   Ⓒ will not leave you when there is trouble   Ⓓ never travels

No. right	1	2	3	4	5	6	7	8
G score	3.0	3.7	4.3	5.1	5.9	6.9	7.7	8.8

42

Most water craft travel through water. One kind travels right above the water. Its secret is its hydrofoils. These thin foils look and act like wings. They are below the hull and hold it up. They are the only part of the craft to move through water.

One hydrofoil boat traveled swiftly in 1918, fifteen years after the first airplane. Its designer was Alexander Graham Bell, the inventor of the telephone.

One such boat is called The Hovercraft. It carries people between England and France. Regular boats travel the same route, but The Hovercraft is faster. It seems to fly right above the water.

1. **The craft in this story travels** Ⓐ right above the water   Ⓑ through the water   Ⓒ under the water   Ⓓ as high as a plane
2. **The foils look and act like**   Ⓐ sails   Ⓑ steering wheels   Ⓒ wings   Ⓓ motors
3. **The part of the craft that moves through the water is the**   Ⓐ hull   Ⓑ foils   Ⓒ sails   Ⓓ motor
4. **England calls one of its hydrofoils**   Ⓐ The High Flyer   Ⓑ The France   Ⓒ The Hovercraft   Ⓓ The Alexander Graham Bell
5. **An early hydrofoil traveled in**   Ⓐ 1850   Ⓑ 1918   Ⓒ 1915   Ⓓ 1970
6. **Alexander Graham Bell invented the**   Ⓐ telephone   Ⓑ airplane   Ⓒ boat   Ⓓ foil wrapping
7. **The Hovercraft travels**   Ⓐ more slowly than regular boats   Ⓑ at the same speed as regular boats   Ⓒ faster than planes   Ⓓ faster than the regular boats
8. **Why is the hydrofoil not really flying?**   Ⓐ the hull is in the water   Ⓑ the foils are in the water   Ⓒ its wings are too small   Ⓓ it doesn't go between airports

No. right	1	2	3	4	5	6	7	8
G score	3.2	3.7	4.4	5.2	6.0	6.9	7.7	8.8

Are you panic proof? Most persons are not. In England someone fell on a stair. Panic followed—178 persons were trampled to death. In Michigan someone fainted. There was a call for water. Someone thought it meant fire—71 were killed. In Oklahoma the beard of a Santa Claus caught on fire—36 died.

To avoid panic you should do your thinking before you become part of a panicky crowd. Here are a few suggestions:

a. As you sit in any crowd, pick out an exit that is not the one where most persons entered, and plan to use it if the need arises.

b. If a rush starts, do not get into it. Stay still. Let it pass. Then go to the exit you have chosen.

c. Do not scream. Speak quietly. Act calmly.

d. Do not stop for your hat and coat unless they are at hand.

e. If there is smoke, crouch, do not crawl, as you go. The best air is about three feet above the floor.

f. When you are out of the building, stay out. Many dead would now be alive if they had not attempted to return for something.

g. When you get out, move far from the door so others can get out.

---

1. **In Michigan a panic was caused by a call** Ⓐ for help Ⓑ of fire Ⓒ for water Ⓓ for a doctor

2. **If you are one of a crowd when panic starts, you should** Ⓐ run with the others Ⓑ stay still until the crowd has passed Ⓒ crouch Ⓓ call for help as loudly as you can

3. **If panic occurs, leave** Ⓐ where everyone entered Ⓑ where you entered Ⓒ through any exit you see Ⓓ where most people did not enter

4. **If there is danger when you are one of a crowd, you should** Ⓐ tell everyone to rush away Ⓑ give the alarm by screaming Ⓒ speak and move quietly Ⓓ find your coat before you leave

5. **When once out of a place where there is panic, you should** Ⓐ return to help others Ⓑ stay outside Ⓒ go back for your coat Ⓓ remain near the exit

6. **If there is smoke in a room, you should** Ⓐ crawl out slowly Ⓑ walk outside Ⓒ run out quickly Ⓓ crouch as you move out

7. **When you are safely outside a burning building, stay far away from the door so that** Ⓐ people may enter Ⓑ others may leave Ⓒ the smoke can get out Ⓓ you will not fall on a stair

8. **Sudden fright needs to be** Ⓐ ignored Ⓑ controlled Ⓒ smothered Ⓓ worn out

No. right	1	2	3	4	5	6	7	8
G score	4.3	4.8	5.4	6.0	6.7	7.4	8.0	8.9

44

In a canoelike foldboat just seventeen feet long, Dr. Hannes Lindemann set out from the Canary Islands to sail alone across the Atlantic Ocean to America.

After several days of sailing westward, he ran into a storm. Soon he was drenched, and his fingers were swollen from bailing water. The sides of the boat bent to every wave. A great wave crashed on top of the frail boat, almost drowning its lone passenger and nearly swamping the canoe. Another wave wrenched away the rudder. Without it he would be forced to paddle to stay on course. Taking a quick dive, he caught hold of a rope tied to the rudder and rescued it.

After the storm was over, dolphins played around his boat, slapping it with their tails. They were chased away by a huge shark.

Days later a worse storm howled around Dr. Lindemann. Waves were mountainous. One turned his boat over, throwing him into the water. Even though he was able to right the vessel, he had lost most of his food.

Now Dr. Lindemann's mind began to wander. He saw things that were not there. He talked to imaginary people. Finally the boat's rudder was swept away, and the man had to paddle to keep on course.

Barely alive, by some miracle he landed on the island of St. Martin.

1. **This story tells about a trip that was** Ⓐ adventurous Ⓑ uneventful Ⓒ important Ⓓ enjoyable
2. **After Dr. Lindemann had been sailing westward several days** Ⓐ a storm arose Ⓑ the sun came up earlier Ⓒ the full moon rose Ⓓ the rains came
3. **This journey was made by a** Ⓐ speed boat Ⓑ canoelike boat Ⓒ steamboat Ⓓ fishing boat
4. **Dr. Lindemann's fingers were swollen from** Ⓐ playing with water Ⓑ carrying water Ⓒ pulling a rope Ⓓ bailing water
5. **What appeared first after the storm was over?** Ⓐ dolphins Ⓑ sharks Ⓒ boats Ⓓ rafts
6. **This voyager lost most of his** Ⓐ money Ⓑ drinking water Ⓒ food Ⓓ clothing
7. **At one point, Dr. Lindemann began to see things and talk to people who were** Ⓐ imagining things Ⓑ wandering Ⓒ in his imagination Ⓓ swept away
8. **The boat lost its** Ⓐ motor Ⓑ sail Ⓒ rudder Ⓓ oars

No. right	1	2	3	4	5	6	7	8
G score	3.4	3.9	4.6	5.3	6.0	6.9	7.7	8.6

One of the most important advances in medicine is the ability to transfuse blood. Countless lives are saved each year because transfusions make certain surgical procedures possible.

When a transfusion is needed and a life is saved, the doctors are not the only heroes. Women and men in all occupations have made this event possible. They have donated some of their own blood. Because they have donated blood to a "blood bank," they do not know the person who has received it. They know only that they have helped another human being.

The Red Cross runs a widely known blood program. A person who wishes to donate blood can do so at a Red Cross center. Trained staff interview each potential donor about his or her health to screen out those whose blood may not be safe for the recipient. Then a pint of blood is taken from each donor's arm. The donor may feel a little weak afterwards, but a doughnut and a cup of coffee are just what the doctor ordered to put them quickly on their feet again.

45

---

1. **This selection is about**   Ⓐ special surgical procedures   Ⓑ donating blood   Ⓒ becoming a Red Cross worker   Ⓓ doctors
2. **Certain surgical procedures require the use of**   Ⓐ doughnuts and coffee   Ⓑ Red Cross centers   Ⓒ all occupations   Ⓓ transfused blood
3. **Which of the following is true?**   Ⓐ the donor always chooses the person who will receive his or her blood   Ⓑ the donor always knows who will receive the blood   Ⓒ the donor is always Red Cross staff.   Ⓓ the donor does not normally know who will receive his or her blood
4. **Why are potential donors screened?**   Ⓐ in some cases, their blood may not be safe   Ⓑ to determine their occupation   Ⓒ to choose future Red Cross staff   Ⓓ so they will not be weak
5. **How might you feel after donating blood?**   Ⓐ extremely ill   Ⓑ a little weak   Ⓒ more energetic   Ⓓ restless
6. **How much blood would be safe to donate at one time?**   Ⓐ one pint   Ⓑ five pints   Ⓒ ten pints   Ⓓ twelve pints
7. **Which of the following does the selection stress?**   Ⓐ many operations are performed each year   Ⓑ doctors are important   Ⓒ you don't have to be a doctor to help save lives   Ⓓ the Red Cross needs more coffee
8. **Blood donors have the satisfaction of**   Ⓐ helping another human being   Ⓑ performing operations   Ⓒ serving doughnuts and coffee   Ⓓ choosing recipients of blood

No. right	1	2	3	4	5	6	7	8
G score	4.0	4.6	5.2	5.9	6.6	7.3	8.0	8.9

46

The United States Army built the worst railroad in the world to train its Army Railway Battalion.

The railroad tracks were laid for 100 miles over the mud and water holes of Louisiana swamps. The rails twisted and squirmed like a snake. The old locomotive wheezed. Every time the train ran, a wrecker followed it. Sometimes the wrecker helped to get the train back on the track, and sometimes the train helped the wrecker.

One trip was made in a downpouring rain. The brakeman, awaking from a nap in the caboose, thought that the train had left the tracks and taken off across the swamp. It took him some time to figure out that the track was all right up front but had sunk out of sight in the mud behind the caboose. On this trip the train went off the track five times and the wrecker three. Fifty hours after starting, Bouncing Betty of the Bayou rattled into the station at the snappy speed of two miles an hour.

1. **How many miles long was this worst railroad in the world?** Ⓐ 10
   Ⓑ 100 Ⓒ 1,000 Ⓓ 10,000
2. **Which country built this railroad?** Ⓐ England Ⓑ Russia
   Ⓒ Germany Ⓓ the United States
3. **In which state was this railroad built?** Ⓐ Mississippi Ⓑ Louisiana
   Ⓒ Alabama Ⓓ Missouri
4. **The tracks were built on land that was** Ⓐ hard Ⓑ smooth
   Ⓒ soft Ⓓ dry
5. **The locomotive used by the Army was** Ⓐ new Ⓑ twisted
   Ⓒ shiny Ⓓ old
6. **The story says one trip was made in a** Ⓐ shower Ⓑ snowstorm
   Ⓒ heavy rain Ⓓ hailstorm
7. **The rails** Ⓐ creaked Ⓑ wheezed Ⓒ rattled Ⓓ squirmed
8. **The brakeman took his nap in the** Ⓐ engine Ⓑ wrecker
   Ⓒ station Ⓓ caboose

No. right	1	2	3	4	5	6	7	8
G score	2.7	3.5	4.1	5.0	5.9	7.0	7.9	9.2

Betty Allen likes to watch her father's bees. Sometimes she sees them coming in with a load of pollen in the pollen baskets on their hind legs. In the spring it may be brown pollen from the pear blossoms; in the summer it may be yellow pollen from the corn tassels. From this pollen the bees make food for the baby bees. It is called beebread.

Betty is not afraid of bees, for she knows they will not sting her if she does not get in their way. It makes them angry if anyone stands in front of the entrance to the hive when they are coming in with a heavy load. She stands off to one side and watches them alight on the board in front of the hive. Some bees are always guarding this entrance. At night after all the bees are in the hive, these guards brush off the board with their front legs.

47

1. **Betty watches the bees carrying** Ⓐ honey Ⓑ wax Ⓒ pollen Ⓓ flowers
2. **The pollen baskets are on their** Ⓐ front legs Ⓑ wings Ⓒ back Ⓓ hind legs
3. **Beebread is made from** Ⓐ pollen Ⓑ honey Ⓒ wax Ⓓ nectar
4. **Pollen from the corn is** Ⓐ brown Ⓑ yellow Ⓒ white Ⓓ green
5. **Bees get pollen from the corn** Ⓐ leaves Ⓑ tassels Ⓒ stalks Ⓓ silks
6. **Pollen from pear blossoms is** Ⓐ brown Ⓑ yellow Ⓒ white Ⓓ green
7. **Bees always guard** Ⓐ the top of the hive Ⓑ the flowers Ⓒ the entrance to the hive Ⓓ the pollen
8. **They brush off the board with** Ⓐ their hind legs Ⓑ their front legs Ⓒ their wings Ⓓ a leaf

No. right	1	2	3	4	5	6	7	8
G score	2.6	3.4	4.1	5.0	5.9	7.0	8.0	9.3

48

In Washington, D.C., the capital of the United States, is a beautiful white marble building called the Lincoln Memorial. It was built by the people of the United States to show their love for Abraham Lincoln. It took ten years to build this memorial, which stands on the bank of the Potomac River. Around the building are thirty-six tall columns. There are thirty-six columns because there were thirty-six states in the United States at the time of Lincoln's death. In the center of the memorial is a large statue of Lincoln seated in a chair looking down at visitors. Many tourists visit the Lincoln Memorial every year to honor the memory of a great American.

1. **Washington is**　Ⓐ a beautiful building　Ⓑ the capital of the United States　Ⓒ the Lincoln Memorial　Ⓓ a marble building
2. **This memorial was built in**　Ⓐ five years　Ⓑ ten years　Ⓒ fifteen years　Ⓓ thirty-six years
3. **There were thirty-six states when**　Ⓐ Lincoln died　Ⓑ the memorial was built　Ⓒ Lincoln was born　Ⓓ Washington was founded
4. **The Lincoln Memorial is a**　Ⓐ city　Ⓑ column　Ⓒ river　Ⓓ building
5. **The Lincoln Memorial was built**　Ⓐ by Abraham Lincoln　Ⓑ by the people of the United States　Ⓒ by Washington　Ⓓ by the French
6. **The Potomac is a**　Ⓐ city　Ⓑ memorial　Ⓒ river　Ⓓ bank
7. **In the statue Lincoln is portrayed**　Ⓐ on horseback　Ⓑ seated　Ⓒ standing　Ⓓ holding a sword
8. **The story says tourists visit the memorial to**　Ⓐ have a picnic　Ⓑ look at the view　Ⓒ write postcards　Ⓓ honor Lincoln's memory

No. right	1	2	3	4	5	6	7	8
G score	2.5	3.3	3.9	4.8	5.8	6.9	8.0	9.4

The city of Venice in Italy is built on thousands of tiny islands. They are connected by a network of bridges. Because all the streets are water, all the vehicles in Venice are boats. The Grand Canal, the main thoroughfare, is as wide as a highway and full of floating traffic. The Ponte di Rialto spans across it. Along this ancient bridge are shops. Merchants have sold trinkets and treasures here for hundreds of years. Another bridge, built between a courthouse and a jail, is called the Bridge of Sighs. Here, prisoners condemned to death caught their last glimpse of their beautiful city.

49

1. **Venice is** Ⓐ an Italian island Ⓑ a network of highways Ⓒ an inland city Ⓓ built on thousands of islands
2. **To get around Venice, you must** Ⓐ take a train Ⓑ take a motorcycle Ⓒ take a boat Ⓓ bicycle
3. **The main waterway in the city is** Ⓐ never crowded Ⓑ wide and busy Ⓒ called the Ponte di Rialto Ⓓ full of treasures
4. **The Ponte di Rialto** Ⓐ is a body of water Ⓑ is a very old bridge Ⓒ spans a highway Ⓓ is a boat
5. **On the Ponte di Rialto, you can buy** Ⓐ boats Ⓑ pizza Ⓒ trinkets Ⓓ signs
6. **The other bridge mentioned** Ⓐ is also on the Grand Canal Ⓑ is called the Bridge of Unhappiness Ⓒ has merchants and shops Ⓓ is built between a courthouse and a jail
7. **It's called the Bridge of Sighs because** Ⓐ of the sorrow of those who crossed it Ⓑ that's the sound the water makes Ⓒ no one likes it Ⓓ it is so old
8. **To get to school, children in Venice probably** Ⓐ span the canal Ⓑ take a school boat Ⓒ go on the main thoroughfare Ⓓ go on the Ponte di Rialto

No. right	1	2	3	4	5	6	7	8
G score	3.3	3.8	4.6	5.5	6.3	7.3	8.2	9.5

50

Many years ago, when people in faraway parts of Alaska were dying because they did not have serum for a throat disease, it was decided to get it to them by dog teams. It was a terrible journey through blinding snow and freezing winds. Relay teams were used, but the last lap was long and the cold extreme. The driver tied skins about the dogs to keep them warm, but the wind cut through and nearly froze them as they ran. The panting dogs breathed so much of the icy air that it injured their lungs. But they struggled on until they reached the town with the precious medicine and saved many people's lives. These dogs were real heroes. Had this happened to-day, the serum would have been delivered in a few hours by a swiftly flying airplane.

---

1. **In what place did these sick people live?** Ⓐ Russia   Ⓑ Iceland   Ⓒ Alaska   Ⓓ Canada

2. **What kind of disease did they have?**   Ⓐ throat   Ⓑ nose   Ⓒ lung   Ⓓ blood

3. **What did they need most for this disease?**   Ⓐ doctors   Ⓑ coal   Ⓒ food   Ⓓ serum

4. **The serum reached the sick people by**   Ⓐ ship   Ⓑ dog team   Ⓒ railroad   Ⓓ airplane

5. **The journey was**   Ⓐ pleasant   Ⓑ terrible   Ⓒ a failure   Ⓓ mountainous

6. **As they ran, the dogs**   Ⓐ dropped   Ⓑ starved   Ⓒ growled   Ⓓ nearly froze

7. **How did the driver try to keep the dogs warm?**   Ⓐ by building fires   Ⓑ by putting blankets on them   Ⓒ by tying skins about them   Ⓓ by making them run

8. **The dogs were heroes because they**   Ⓐ hurt their lungs   Ⓑ nearly froze   Ⓒ saved lives   Ⓓ lived in Alaska

---

No. right	1	2	3	4	5	6	7	8
G score	2.8	3.6	4.3	5.2	6.2	7.2	8.3	9.6

Once I had a duck that laid six eggs, but paid no attention to them. I also had a hen that wanted to set, so I placed the duck's eggs in the hen's nest. The hen could not tell a duck egg from a hen egg, so she sat on the six eggs. Five of them hatched as fluffy ducklings. Perhaps the hen could not tell a duckling from a chick either. Anyway, she seemed to love them.

One day when I was eating lunch I heard the mother hen loudly clucking. She seemed to be in great trouble. I thought that a hawk might be trying to catch her little ones. I rushed out of the house, at the same time yelling at the top of my voice to frighten the hawk away. Then I burst out laughing. The mother hen was running up and down on the bank of the brook, clucking and scolding while her five baby ducklings were having a merry time swimming and diving in the water!

1. **What was the first thing the hen wanted to do?**   Ⓐ set   Ⓑ cluck   Ⓒ scold   Ⓓ swim
2. **How many eggs were there?**   Ⓐ 4   Ⓑ 6   Ⓒ 7   Ⓓ 12
3. **How many eggs failed to hatch?**   Ⓐ 1   Ⓑ 5   Ⓒ 6   Ⓓ 7
4. **What kind of eggs were they?**   Ⓐ hen eggs   Ⓑ hawk eggs   Ⓒ chicken eggs   Ⓓ duck eggs
5. **Where was the hen when she was scolding?**   Ⓐ on the nest   Ⓑ on the bank   Ⓒ in the brook   Ⓓ in the house
6. **The hen was scolding because**   Ⓐ of the yelling   Ⓑ the ducklings were in the water   Ⓒ a hawk was about to catch her babies   Ⓓ the ducklings were not chicks
7. **Who were having a merry time?**   Ⓐ ducklings   Ⓑ hens   Ⓒ hawks   Ⓓ chicks
8. **When the ducklings were in the water, the mother hen felt**   Ⓐ amused   Ⓑ merry   Ⓒ unhappy   Ⓓ fierce

No. right	1	2	3	4	5	6	7	8
G score	2.7	3.5	4.3	5.2	6.2	7.3	8.5	9.9

52

Admiral Byrd and other explorers who ventured into the far Arctic and Antarctic regions had to take great risks. Here is a true story about the Antarctic explorer Ernest Shackleton.

An Antarctic storm dashed him and a small crew onto an icy shore. A mountain covered with snow and ice stood between them and any help. They toiled up the mountain. The night was very dark, and a gale was blowing by the time they reached the top. What lay down the other side of the mountain they did not know, nor could they see. Perhaps deep gorges lay below, but down they must go, and quickly, or they would freeze. They coiled their ropes for sleds, sat down, linked arms, and started sliding to life or death. Soon they were going a mile a minute. Because their slide ended in a soft snowdrift at the foot of the mountain, they lived to tell this tale.

1. **This story tells about the explorers'** Ⓐ health Ⓑ humor Ⓒ courage Ⓓ families
2. **The story tells of an adventure** Ⓐ by Byrd Ⓑ by Shackleton Ⓒ in the Arctic Ⓓ in wintertime
3. **This adventure happened in the** Ⓐ Arctic Ⓑ Atlantic Ⓒ Pacific Ⓓ Antarctic
4. **Because of the storm, the explorers were** Ⓐ at the top of the mountain Ⓑ separated Ⓒ stranded Ⓓ lost at sea
5. **To reach help, the leader and his crew were forced to** Ⓐ run for miles Ⓑ climb a mountain Ⓒ jump deep gorges Ⓓ blow their boat whistles
6. **These explorers' sleds were made of** Ⓐ steel Ⓑ wood and steel Ⓒ rope Ⓓ wood and rope
7. **The men landed** Ⓐ in a stream of water Ⓑ on a lake of ice Ⓒ on top of a house Ⓓ in a soft snowdrift
8. **Adventure of this kind is** Ⓐ frequent Ⓑ thrilling Ⓒ sad Ⓓ amusing

No. right	1	2	3	4	5	6	7	8
G score	3.5	4.1	4.7	5.6	6.5	7.3	8.2	9.3

The second day of the rodeo was nearing its close. The July sun was hot. The heat seemed intensified by the clouds of dust that rose over the field. The crowd tried in vain to cool itself by buying the wares of the soda-pop boy. In one corner the cattle huddled with lowered heads in pitiful endurance of the sun's rays. One last event held the spectators. Edwin Barnett, a fourteen-year-old boy, was to ride a wild Brahman steer. The great moment arrived. The gates were thrown open. The crowd seemed to strain forward in anticipation. The steer, with its youthful rider, raced frantically from the chute in an effort to rid himself of this clinging burden. He reared and plunged wildly and was made more frantic by the desperate realization that he could not free himself. The crowd watched breathlessly. Would the boy be able to ride him? The steer made one last jump and, with a savage bellow, broke into a long-gaited run toward the herd, but the boy clung on fearlessly.

The judges gave the command to take him off. The crowd sank back. The steer had been ridden, and the boy had won. Texas had one more cowboy.

53

1. **What do you think would be the best title for this incident?** Ⓐ A Texas Rodeo   Ⓑ The Fourth of July Celebration   Ⓒ A Barbecue   Ⓓ Away Down South
2. **At what season of the year did this rodeo take place?** Ⓐ winter   Ⓑ summer   Ⓒ spring   Ⓓ fall
3. **What is a rodeo?** Ⓐ a hot day   Ⓑ a bullfight   Ⓒ a merry-go-round at a fair   Ⓓ a meet where wild steers and horses are ridden
4. **This story says that the crowd tried to cool itself by** Ⓐ sitting in the shade   Ⓑ buying cold drinks   Ⓒ fanning   Ⓓ going in bathing
5. **When the steer finally realized he could not get rid of his burden, what did he do? He** Ⓐ fell down   Ⓑ rushed madly toward the crowd   Ⓒ ran toward the herd   Ⓓ huddled with lowered head
6. **The Brahman steer was** Ⓐ fearless   Ⓑ breathless   Ⓒ wild   Ⓓ huddled in one corner
7. **The judges commanded that the boy be taken off the steer because** Ⓐ the boy had won   Ⓑ it was the close of day   Ⓒ the boy was frightened   Ⓓ the boy was hurt
8. **The crowd sank back because they were** Ⓐ hot   Ⓑ long-gaited   Ⓒ relieved that the boy was all right   Ⓓ desperate

No. right	1	2	3	4	5	6	7	8
G score	4.1	4.7	5.4	6.1	6.9	7.6	8.6	9.5

54

Many people think that Frankenstein was a monster. They are wrong. The novel, *Frankenstein,* was written in 1818 by Mary Wollstonecraft Shelley. It tells the story of a scientist named Count Frankenstein and how he created a monster from the parts of dead bodies. The monster has no name in the book.

In the beginning, the monster was kind. It tried to fit in with other people. The people hated it because it was so ugly, so the monster began to hate people. Finally, it turned to murder. The monster killed Count Frankenstein and disappeared.

Many films have been made about Frankenstein's monster, but few, if any, are like Mary Wollstonecraft Shelley's character.

1. **Frankenstein was a**   Ⓐ monster   Ⓑ man   Ⓒ writer   Ⓓ woman
2. *Frankenstein* **appeared in**   Ⓐ 1818   Ⓑ 1918   Ⓒ 1819   Ⓓ 1776
3. **The monster's name was**   Ⓐ Frankenstein   Ⓑ Wollstonecraft
   Ⓒ unknown   Ⓓ Shelley
4. **The monster hated people because**   Ⓐ it was mean   Ⓑ a man created
   him   Ⓒ it was ugly   Ⓓ people hated it
5. **The monster wanted**   Ⓐ to be friendly   Ⓑ to be a scientist   Ⓒ to be
   in films   Ⓓ to murder the author
6. **The book was written by**   Ⓐ Percy Bysshe Shelley   Ⓑ Count
   Frankenstein   Ⓒ Shelley Berman   Ⓓ Mary Wollstonecraft Shelley
7. **The monster was created from**   Ⓐ dead bats   Ⓑ one dead body
   Ⓒ dead bodies   Ⓓ living people
8. *Frankenstein* **is**   Ⓐ a true story   Ⓑ fiction   Ⓒ an article
   Ⓓ a scientific report

No. right	1	2	3	4	5	6	7	8
G score	2.2	2.6	3.5	4.6	5.7	7.0	8.4	10.0

Anteaters' tongues are 18 inches long. They don't have any teeth, but then they don't need any. Their mouths are long like a tube to contain this interesting tongue.

An anteater doesn't just eat ants; it eats many kinds of insects that live in the ground, under rocks, and in trees. It uses the third digit on its foot to dig into nests of insects. This toe has a very powerful claw on it that makes it easy for the anteater to break into termites' nests. Once it has dug open a nest it uses its sticky tongue to trap the insects.

The largest anteaters live in South and Central America. They can be up to four feet long, not including the tail which can also be 4 feet long. The animal is completely terrestrial which means it never goes in the water. It can live for a long time without eating.

1. **An anteater** Ⓐ only eats ants Ⓑ eats ants and other insects Ⓒ eats only termites Ⓓ eats water bugs
2. **The tongue of this animal can be up to** Ⓐ 10 inches long Ⓑ 12 inches long Ⓒ 20 inches long Ⓓ 18 inches long
3. **In this selection, the word digit is used meaning** Ⓐ a number Ⓑ a toe Ⓒ a claw Ⓓ a tongue
4. **The largest anteaters live** Ⓐ on the Mississippi River Ⓑ in Africa Ⓒ in Alaska Ⓓ in South and Central America
5. **The insects are trapped by the anteater's tongue because** Ⓐ it is like a vacuum cleaner Ⓑ it curls around them Ⓒ it is sticky Ⓓ it smashes them
6. **The word terrestrial means** Ⓐ to live only on the ground Ⓑ to live only in the water Ⓒ to live in the water and on the ground Ⓓ to live in the trees
7. **Without food an anteater could** Ⓐ die in one day Ⓑ last a long time Ⓒ die in an hour Ⓓ live for two years
8. **An anteater's mouth is** Ⓐ short with many teeth Ⓑ long with many teeth Ⓒ long with no teeth Ⓓ short with no teeth

No. right	1	2	3	4	5	6	7	8
G score	3.4	4.0	4.8	5.8	6.8	7.8	9.0	10.2

56

People marked the passage of minutes and hours without watches. How do you think they kept a record of days and months without a calendar?

Since the time from the highest position of the sun one day to its highest position the next day always seemed the same, they called this amount of time one day. Since the time from one full moon to the next full moon always appeared the same, they called this amount of time one lunar month. There were about 28 days in a lunar month. At present, the month is divided into about 4 weeks, the week into 7 days, the day into 24 hours, the hour into 60 minutes, and the minute into 60 seconds.

1. **From full moon to full moon is about** Ⓐ one day Ⓑ one week Ⓒ four weeks Ⓓ two months
2. **The calendar keeps a record of** Ⓐ hours Ⓑ minutes Ⓒ months Ⓓ seconds
3. **There are twenty-four hours from** Ⓐ sunrise to sunset Ⓑ sunset to sunset Ⓒ full moon to full moon Ⓓ sunset to sunrise
4. **What kind of month is described?** Ⓐ calendar Ⓑ lunar Ⓒ solar Ⓓ stellar
5. **How many times does the sun rise in a week?** Ⓐ four Ⓑ seven Ⓒ thirty Ⓓ sixty
6. **Which played the most important part in indicating days and months?** Ⓐ heavenly bodies Ⓑ sundials and shadows Ⓒ clocks Ⓓ watches
7. **Minutes are divided into** Ⓐ days Ⓑ months Ⓒ hours Ⓓ seconds
8. **How many days were in a month?** Ⓐ twenty-four Ⓑ approximately 28 Ⓒ sixty Ⓓ 7

No. right	1	2	3	4	5	6	7	8
G score	3.8	4.5	5.2	6.0	6.9	7.6	8.6	9.8

Have you heard of the Devil's Triangle? This triangle is made up of part of the Atlantic Ocean and the sky above it. It is located between Bermuda and the southeast coast of the U.S. It is also called the Bermuda Triangle, the Mystery Triangle, and the Triangle of Death. According to some people, very mysterious things happen here. These people say that these mysterious happenings are caused by the devil or by beings from outer space.

It is true that many ships and planes have disappeared in this region. This fact, however, is not surprising. There is a lot of traffic here. Ships and planes going between the United States and Africa, Europe, and South America all pass through. In addition, the weather can change very quickly. Dangerous storms start with little warning. Finally, the Gulf Stream runs through the Triangle. This mighty ocean current can cause very large waves, again with little warning.

Although the Bermuda Triangle can be dangerous, its dangers can be explained by science.

57

1. **The Devil's Triangle is located between Bermuda and** Ⓐ the southeast coast of Africa Ⓑ New York Ⓒ Europe Ⓓ the southeast coast of the U.S.
2. **According to the author,** Ⓐ few ships have disappeared in the Triangle Ⓑ few airplanes have disappeared in the Triangle Ⓒ many ships have disappeared in the Triangle Ⓓ a surprising number of ships have disappeared in the Triangle
3. **The weather in the Triangle** Ⓐ is always stormy Ⓑ changes quickly Ⓒ is usually calm Ⓓ can't be explained
4. **The Gulf Stream** Ⓐ can cause large waves Ⓑ can carry ships away Ⓒ can cause dangerous storms Ⓓ does not go through the Triangle
5. **How many scientific reasons does the author give for ships disappearing in the Triangle?** Ⓐ three Ⓑ four Ⓒ five Ⓓ none
6. **The author feels that if the number of ships in the Triangle increases** Ⓐ more ships will disappear Ⓑ we will know more about the region Ⓒ the devil will sink more Ⓓ more lives will be saved
7. **According to the author, it can be dangerous to fly through the Triangle because of** Ⓐ the Gulf Stream Ⓑ the number of ships Ⓒ dangerous storms Ⓓ large waves
8. **Which of the following names for the Triangle do you think the author thinks is best?** Ⓐ The Devil's Triangle Ⓑ The Bermuda Triangle Ⓒ The Mystery Triangle Ⓓ The Triangle of Death

No. right	1	2	3	4	5	6	7	8
G score	3.7	4.3	5.1	5.9	6.9	7.7	8.8	9.9

58

One of the greatest mysteries of this generation is what is now known as UFOs. UFOs have been seen by thousands of persons and for many hundreds of years. They have been seen by radar and have been photographed. Some are shaped like a thick, inverted saucer, some like a cigar, and some like an egg. Apparently they can stand still in the air or dart off at amazing speeds. Playfully, they have flown circles around our fastest jet planes.

A huge, egg-shaped something about 300 feet long and nearly as bright as our sun, was seen at three o'clock one Sunday morning by a two-man jeep patrol that guards the area where the first atom bomb was exploded. Watching from three miles away, they saw this "something" come down until it was about 50 feet above the atom-bomb bunkers. Then suddenly its light went out.

Some 17 hours later, another military-police patrol saw a similar something hovering just above the earth in the same area. Before they could reach it, the strange something took off into the sky at a 45-degree angle. High in the sky, it blinked its light on and off and then disappeared.

1. **UFOs have been sighted** Ⓐ for thousands of years Ⓑ hundreds of years Ⓒ only by patrols Ⓓ only in this generation
2. **Some are shaped like** Ⓐ bunkers Ⓑ jeeps Ⓒ jet planes Ⓓ plates
3. **One Sunday afternoon, an egg-shaped UFO was seen by** Ⓐ radar Ⓑ a photographer Ⓒ military police Ⓓ people in the bunkers
4. **What were the men in the jeep doing?** Ⓐ searching for UFOs Ⓑ guarding the site of the first atom bomb explosion Ⓒ driving to the atom-bomb bunkers Ⓓ patrolling for jet planes
5. **The UFO they saw was** Ⓐ exploded Ⓑ photographed Ⓒ like a thick, inverted saucer Ⓓ very bright
6. **Some UFOs** Ⓐ land on the bunkers Ⓑ stand still in the air Ⓒ guard the area Ⓓ carry atomic bombs
7. **UFOs are** Ⓐ proven facts Ⓑ military Ⓒ mysteries Ⓓ like cigars and cigarettes
8. **Some UFOs are said to** Ⓐ move at very fast speeds Ⓑ have 45-degree angles Ⓒ hover for 17 hours Ⓓ watch from 3 miles away

No. right	1	2	3	4	5	6	7	8
G score	4.0	4.6	5.5	6.3	7.2	8.1	9.2	10.2

Having devoured many victims, a tiger crouched to spring upon a fox.

"You will not dare to touch me," protested the latter. "I have been created the king of all beasts. If you don't believe me, allow me to trot in front of you. See if the beasts will not run away for fear of me."

The tiger agreed to this, followed the fox, and actually saw all the animals run away before them. It never occurred to him that they were terrified by his own presence. He was coaxed into believing that what the fox said had come true.

1. **The fox told the tiger that he was**   Ⓐ the emperor of all foxes   Ⓑ a king's pet   Ⓒ the king of all beasts   Ⓓ smarter than the tiger

2. **The fox saved his life by**   Ⓐ running away   Ⓑ fighting   Ⓒ asking for mercy   Ⓓ using tactics

3. **In response to the fox's protest, the tiger**   Ⓐ killed him   Ⓑ laughed at him   Ⓒ followed him   Ⓓ ran away from him

4. **The tiger saw**   Ⓐ all other foxes run away   Ⓑ all tigers run away   Ⓒ all birds fly away   Ⓓ all beasts run away

5. **All the animals were terrified by the presence of the**   Ⓐ fox   Ⓑ victims   Ⓒ tiger   Ⓓ hunter

6. **If the tiger had known the truth he would have**   Ⓐ run away   Ⓑ fought   Ⓒ befriended the fox   Ⓓ devoured the fox

7. **We may infer from the story that the tiger is inferior to the fox in**   Ⓐ appearance   Ⓑ strength   Ⓒ ability to run   Ⓓ shrewdness

8. **The story is**   Ⓐ a bit of history   Ⓑ an account of facts   Ⓒ a fable   Ⓓ a newspaper report

No. right	1	2	3	4	5	6	7	8
G score	4.4	5.1	5.9	6.7	7.5	8.4	9.5	10.4

60

About one thousand guests at the Alabama Space and Rocket Center helped one of America's space pioneers celebrate a birthday. The cake was made from red gelatin and was topped with bananas and strawberries.

Deborah Anderson of the Space and Rocket Center staff spoke of the guest of honor, who rode a Jupiter rocket on a 10,000 mile-an-hour suborbital journey May 28, 1959. "Of course, no one is really sure of the day Miss Baker was born," she said, "but we like to give her a birthday party every year to mark her getting older and the advances we've made in space."

Miss Baker is a squirrel monkey. She lives with her mate, George, in a plastic cage on view to visitors touring the museum, which is only a few miles from the Marshall Space Flight Center where the Jupiter rocket was built.

1. **The birthday party was for** Ⓐ Deborah Anderson Ⓑ the Jupiter rocket Ⓒ Miss Baker Ⓓ an astronaut named George
2. **When was Miss Baker born?** Ⓐ May 28, 1959 Ⓑ twenty years ago Ⓒ the same day the Jupiter rocket was built Ⓓ no one knows exactly
3. **Miss Baker flew** Ⓐ 1,000 miles Ⓑ ten thousand miles per hour Ⓒ from the Alabama Space and Rocket Center to the moon Ⓓ 10,000 miles
4. **Miss Baker is *not* one of these:** Ⓐ a space pioneer Ⓑ a squirrel Ⓒ a guest of honor Ⓓ a monkey
5. **Where does George live?** Ⓐ at Marshall Space Flight Center Ⓑ on Jupiter Ⓒ with Deborah Anderson Ⓓ in a cage in a museum
6. **At the birthday party** Ⓐ there was a special cake with fruit Ⓑ Miss Baker was given a plastic cage Ⓒ 10,000 guests were invited Ⓓ a Jupiter rocket was sent into orbit
7. **A party is given every year** Ⓐ to mark the progress made in space Ⓑ to celebrate Alabama's Space and Rocket Center Ⓒ to welcome visitors to the museum Ⓓ to honor George's suborbital journey
8. **Choose the best title:** Ⓐ Animals Help Science Ⓑ Curious George Goes into Space Ⓒ A U.S. Space Pioneer Marks a Birthday Ⓓ How the Jupiter Rocket Made History

No. right	1	2	3	4	5	6	7	8
G score	4.2	4.8	5.7	6.6	7.4	8.4	9.5	10.5